Science in Elite Sport

Science in Elite Sport

Edited by

E. Müller
University of Salzburg

F. Ludescher
Federal State Tyrol

and

G. Zallinger
University of Salzburg

E & FN Spon
An imprint of Routledge

First published 1999
by E & FN Spon, an imprint of Routledge
11 New Fetter Lane, London EC4P 4EE

Simultaneously published in the USA and Canada
by Routledge
29 West 35th Street, New York, NY 10001

Printed and bound in Great Britain by
Biddles Ltd, Guildford and King's Lynn

Publisher's Note
This book has been prepared from camera-ready provided by the editors.

British Library Cataloguing in Publication Data
A catalogue record for this book is available
from the British Library

ISBN 0 419 24530 8

Science in Elite Sport

"International Symposium on Sciences for Training in Sport - Requirements and Opportunities for Achieving Optimum Synergies for the Athlete"

March 13-15, 1998
Innsbruck, Igls
Austria

Scientific Committee
Erich MÜLLER (Chair)
Alfred AIGNER
Peter BAUMGARTL
Friedrich FETZ
Helmut HÖRTNAGL
Werner KANDOLF
Elmar KORNEXL
Günther MITTERBAUER
Werner NACHBAUER
Ernst RAAS

Organizing Committee
Friedl LUDESCHER (Chair)
Rainer GERZABEK
Daniela MÄNNEL
Wolfgang MÜLLER
Harald PERNITSCH
Klaus WEITHAS
Gerhard ZALLINGER

Contents

Introduction

The international Eurathlon Symposium 'Science in Elite Sport' was held in Innsbruck/Igls, Austria, from March, 13–15, 1998. This congress was supported by the European Union and was organized by ABS, an association for supporting elite sports.

The scientific program offered a broad spectrum of current research work in elite sport and gave a an interesting overview on the various models of scientific services in elite sport in different European countries.

Apart from the scientific program, numerous social activities provided many opportunities to make friends and to enjoy spring in the Alps. Thanks to the support of numerous public institutions especially the federal states Tyrol, Vorarlberg and Salzburg as well as the Federal Government and various sponsors we were in a position to offer also some attractive joint events.

In the proceedings of this congress, the three keynotes and ten invited oral presentations are published. We hope that this congress report will stimulate many of our colleagues throughout the world to intensify the research field in elite sport and to initiate a closer and more intensive cooperation among scientists, athletes, and coaches.

Erich Müller, Chair
Friedl Ludescher
Gerhard Zallinger

We would like to express our cordial thanks to Ingrid and Andreas Sandmayr for the time and energy they invested in the editing of this book and to Kirk Allison for editing and translating the various contributions to this volume.

1
THE DEMAND PROFILE OF MODERN HIGH-PERFORMANCE TRAINING

E. MÜLLER, C. RASCHNER and H. SCHWAMEDER
University of Salzburg

Keywords: Austria, biomechanics, demand profile, planing of training, ski jumping, sport-specific variables of influence, technique-specific strength training, tennis, training devices, training science.

1 Introduction

Although an enormously high level of achievement could be reached in high performance sport for nearly every sport type, the end of performance development is not yet in sight. Even when performance improvements are realized in ever smaller increments, one can assume that they will continue in all sports a long time into the future. In the future improvements at the international level in performance may well proceed above all on the basis of improvements in the quality of training and not so much from an increase in the scope of training.

High achievement sport has developed internationally into an economically significant phenomenon. International events such as the Olympic Games or world championships are central media events. Consequently the phenomenon of high performance sport has also become very interesting from a scientific point of view, confirmed by the great number of training science and sport-medical conferences and publications. Training science has become an integrative science which systematically collects knowledge from numerous mother disciplines such as medicine, psychology, physics, chemistry, biology, etc.; from these it derives theories for sport performance level optimization. Sport training can thus be defined as a scientifically grounded, purposeful activity characterized by the pursuit of performance optimization. Then the systematically planned training process can reach a high level of quality when the following steps are observed in the manner of a control circuit system (cf. Fig. 1):

- exactly define the training goals to be achieved;
- select individual training methods from the latest state of training science

research and plan these in detail;
- structure training according to the training plan;
- check the development of performance in regular intervals for all essential variables of influence, and
- interpret the results of performance checks and adapt the training plan correspondingly.

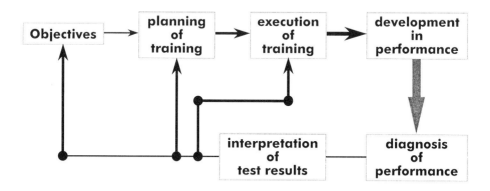

Fig. 1.   Model for training quality optimization.

Performance checks obviously have a very high place value in modern elite sport training. Continuous directing and controlling of the training process is of central significance to avoid wrong tracks and by this guarantee a high level of training economy. Efficient performance checks, however, pre-suppose testing procedures of high quality. They must satisfy the criteria of objectivity, reliability and validity to a particular degree.

Sport performance diagnostics, however, are of significance not only for directing the training process in the narrow sense of the word. The exact determination of training goals presupposes that performance-determining variables of influence, or their levels of influence, respectively, are known as exactly as possible. This holds true for technical, tactical, conditioning and psychological subgoals. In many cases, these can be determined only by means of performance-diagnostic procedures.

Training science literature contains numerous studies which demonstrate that the training involved in general conditioning, valid for all forms of sport, leads to considerable improvements in particular physical parameters. However, training of this kind hardly succeeds in increasing competitive capacity. On the other hand, it was possible to show in many cases that the use of technique-specific means of training - parallel to general conditioning training - leads to considerable improvements in performance also among athletes with many years of training experience (BOSCO 1985; HAKKINEN/ KOMI 1985; MÜLLER/WACHTER 1989; SALE 1993; ZATSIORSKY 1996; SIFF/VERKHOSHANSKY 1996).

It seems to be generally accepted that organismic adaptability increases with a reduction in the number of adaptive factors, as we must assume a relative limit in organismic adaptability reserves (BOIKO 1989). It is consequently important to direct one's attention to developing highly specific means of training.

Training-scientific investigations likewise indicate that use of rapid turn-around information systems in directing many technical, tactical, conditioning and psychological training goals leads to the shortest possible acquisition time. Rapid turn-around information systems are understood to be performance procedures, mostly controlled by electronics, which are able to make results from training trials available within a few seconds.

The present contribution uses a number of concrete examples to show how training-scientific knowledge can contribute to quality improvement in modern elite sport training. First explored is the significance of planing training long-term. Pedagogical, medical and training-methodological aspects necessitate a carefully structured, developmentally appropriate course of training. A subsequent chapter will extensively address the significance of sport-specific training. Procedures for analyzing performance-determining characteristics are likewise introduced in this as well as those for developing specific procedures for performance diagnostics and the most efficient methods for guiding training goals.

2 Long-term, developmentally appropriate planing of training

Top sports performances are possible generally only after 10 to 15 years of consequent training. Already from early childhood on, one should systematically attend to the development of the specific variables of influence of the respective sport. In childhood and youth the principles of motor development should receive particular attention. As an orientation aid, a long-term training plan divided into segments should be developed for each type of sport. Such should indicate the central training goals for the most important development stages and include entries addressing the scope of training, training methods and means of training. Fig. 2 depicts the basic structure of a long-term training plan for male tennis players which was produced in collaboration with the Austrian Tennis Federation. This drew on numerous insights from investigations concerning performance-determining characteristics for tennis and from the motor development of internationally successful tennis players.

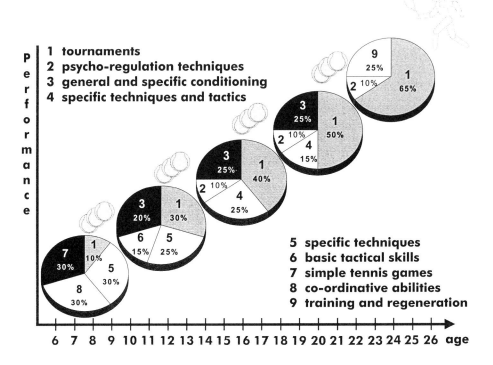

Fig. 2.   Long-term training plan for male tennis players.

Alongside general guidelines of the long-term training plan, age and performance-specific benchmarks for the most important performance characteristics of the particular sport can also be made available. However, such benchmarks can be obtained for the respective sport only after painstaking investigations of numerous athletes at various ages. Thus, for example, for tennis conditioning training, an age- and sex-specific demand and conditioning capacity profile were generated after a ten-year longitudinal study in which all cohort players of the Austrian Tennis Federation between the ages of 10 and 19 were tested, (cf. Fig. 3). Similar orientation values are available in track and field, weightlifting and skiing (SIFF/VERKHOS-HANSKY 1996). However, due to the investigational time expenditure involved, training science can offer such models of investigations only in individual cases.

TESTS \ AGE	11		13		15		17		19	
	male	female	male	female	male	female	male	female	male	female
20m-sprint (s)	3,45-3,65	3,56-3,76	3,28-3,48	3,45-3,65	3,15-3,35	3,41-3,61	3,05-3,25	3,40-3,60	3,02-3,22	3,46-3,66
jump (cm)	26,3-36,3	25,2-34,6	29,9-39,9	26,9-36,3	33,8-43,8	28,2-37,6	36,4-46,4	29,1-38,5	37,5-47,5	29,7-39,1
power (throwing) (m)	13,7-18,1	11,4-15,4	16,5-20,9	14,0-18,0	19,1-23,5	16,5-20,5	22,4-26,8	17,6-21,6	23,6-28,0	18,8-22,8
shuttle run (s)	13,8-15,2	14,0-15,4	12,8-14,2	13,3-14,7	12,0-13,4	13,0-14,4	11,5-12,9	12,7-13,1	11,4-12,8	12,2-13,6
side-steps (s)	13,5-14,9	14,2-15,6	12,8-14,3	13,3-14,7	11,9-13,3	12,8-14,2	11,6-13,0	12,5-13,9	12,5-13,9	12,4-13,8
Fmax hand (N)	170-300	160-260	260-380	250-350	350-470	290-390	440-560	310-410	480-600	350-450
Cooper-Test (m)	2370-2770	2300-2600	2560-2960	2430-2730	2800-3200	2500-2800	2960-3360	2560-2860	2970-3370	2600-2900

Fig. 3.   Age and sex-specific demand profile of conditioning capacity for tennis.

Likewise in selecting training methods one needs to attend particularly to the aspect of developmental appropriateness. On the one hand, following the principle of variation, training exercises and training methods must be varied in regular intervals in order to be able to reach long-term performance improvements; on the other, the organismic load capacity of the child or youth must be taken into account in selecting the practice regimen. Jumping power training for track and field disciplines can be cited as an example: Following the Verkhosansky's model, one initially begins with different jumping exercises for improving intermuskular coordination. In late youth one begins dumbbell training with heavy weights and only after many years of training does deep jump training, which heavily loads the organism, come into play (SIFF/VERKHOSHANSKY 1996).

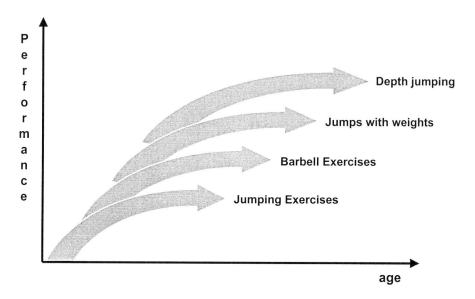

Fig. 4.   Model of a developmentally appropriate construction of jumping power training
          according to VERKHOSANSKY.

Responsibly conceived educational models in elite sport also pursue the integration of school and occupational training into elite sport training. In various European countries the model of sport concentration schools have proven themselves. In this Austria has particularly played a leading role. In this small European country there are over 100 schools in which sports education has particular emphasis. Several of these have concentrated on specific sports (e.g. the skiing Gymnasium in Stams for sport skiers) and coordinate together in sport matters with trainers of the school educational program. Visitors or graduates of these schools are able already to achieve significant successes internationally.

3 Training process specificity

Belonging to the essential characteristics of modern elite sport training are directing the content of the training process according to sport-specific demands. For example, while the general content of power and endurance training with transfer into the competitive situation of the respective sport had stood in the foreground in conditioning training, the new theory proposes that training should simulate sporting movements as closely as possible with regard to the movement pattern, velocity, force-time curve, type of muscle contraction and so forth (SIFF/VERKHOSHANSKY 1996, 20).

To realize a training procedure which is highly oriented towards competition in a specific sport, the following conditions necessarily must be fulfilled:

- Knowledge of the specific parameters relevant to performance in the specific sport or discipline,
- Tests which fully cover sport-specific parameters, and which allow for the classification of test results,
- Training methods and exercises, which fulfill the standard criteria for the specific means of training.

3.1 Procedures for determining sport-specific variables of influence

In the actual practice of training it can be shown again and again that determining sport-specific variables of influence and thus central training goals is built on knowledge from experience and speculation. Scientifically secured knowledge concerning performance-determining characteristics is present only in a few sports (BARTLETT 1977). This may well be attributable to the fact that the analysis of performance-relevant characteristics of a sport generally requires high value, complex measurement equipment. Additionally, field measurements, predominantly under competitive or similar conditions, are what lead to usable results. In this context, computer and video-supported systems have proven themselves for some time for game and contact sport analysis, kinematic, kinetic and electromyographic methods for technical and load analysis as well as physiological and biochemical procedures for determining cardiopulmonary and metabolic characteristics.

3.1.1 Computer-supported game and contact sport analysis

Game and contact sports are characterized by a multiplicity of performance-determining characteristics. Not only the conditioning but above all also the technical-tactical demand levels are complex and involve a number of disciplines. Hence particularly efficient training in these sport types is guaranteed only when strict concentration on individual deficits can take place in the selection of training content. The precondition for this is first an analysis of the actual international performance level for the respective sports. As a consequence, computer and video-supported systems have been developed in past years by several working groups which make possible a complex understanding of essential actions during competition (FERRAUTI/ WEBER 1991; LAMES 1991; LAMES 1994; ZIMMERMANN 1995;

FRÖHNER 1995; REILLY et al. 1993; BERNWICK/MÜLLER 1995a, b; LOY 1995; MÜLLER/LORENZ 1996).

A system developed for tennis guarantees the recording of all important actions of a player during an entire match (BERNWICK/MÜLLER 1995a, b). By means of modern computer technology each individual stroke of an observed player is recorded whereby the respective shot technique (serve, return, volley, stop, etc.), the spin of the ball (drive, topspin, slice), the path of flight (both initial and landing position of balls on the court) and the result of the action (point, error, forced, unforced, etc.) are input. The evaluation software produces a game protocol in which all actions are listed in chronological order, a short analysis serving the trainer as comprehensible rapid mean information directly after the match and finally a comprehensive stroke and error analysis.

Use of this system produced a broadly based, representative norm profile of increased quality for current international elite men's tennis . For this, a total of 200 games by ATP elite players have been analyzed (109 games by the Top 10 players, 39 games ATP 11 - 20 and 52 games ATP > 20). The norm profiles were produced for various performance classes and court surfaces. They describe meaned stroke frequencies, point and error distributions for all stroke categories and various quotients and indices.

As an example, several results of this study are presented here. Fig. 5 depicts the average distribution for individual stroke techniques on two different court surfaces by Top 10 players. The percentage of baseline strokes on clay, 43.2 percent of all strokes, is significantly larger than for hard courts with only 24 percent. While on clay courts baseline strokes and the serve are dominant, serve, return and baseline strokes on hard courts share a nearly equal percentage by which the volley and overhead smash also increase in significance.

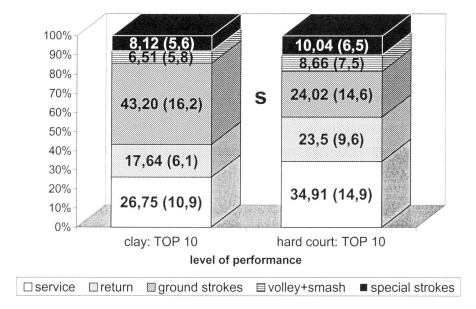

Fig. 5.   Percent distribution of Top 10 player stroke techniques on clay and hard court surfaces.

For example, return stroke technique appears to be of great significance on clay. There are significant differences between Top 10 players and those carrying an ATP ranking between 11 and 20 in the number of mishits and strongly significant differences in favor of Top 10 players in the success quotient (the ratio of points to errors) and in the initiative index (attempts to win points directly with this stroke).

Also with baseline strokes, the effectiveness index - (points - errors) x 100/n - appears to be an especially predictive parameter. As seen in Fig. 6, differences in the three performance classes on clay court are respectively significant to strongly significant while on hard courts, ATP players ranked higher than 20 have significantly less effectiveness than Top 20 players for baseline strokes.

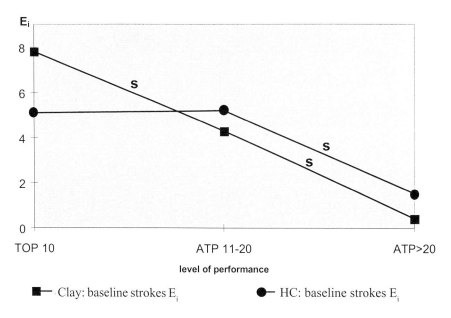

Fig. 6.   Effectiveness index for baseline strokes by 3 performance groups on clay and
          hard court surfaces.

On average 10.09 percent of total shots on clay and 16.60 percent on
hard court comprise attack balls. An attack generally means the player
moves to the net either with a forehand or backhand shot or serve. If a
player scores a direct or „normal" point one speaks of a successfully
concluded attack. For an error, the attack is unsuccessful. On clay an average
of 20.6 percent of attacks (hard court 25.83 percent) result in a direct point;
25.8 percent (hard court: 31.9 percent) are errors.

3.1.2 Biomechanical technique analyses
Descriptive biomechanical analyses attempt to quantitatively characterize
athletes' movement techniques using kinematic, kinetic and
electromyographic methods. The results of such investigations in many
cases have already lead to a better understanding of movements used and
provided trainers valuable support in directing training goals. Given the
enormously high measurement-technical expense involved, for the most
part investigations have mainly concerned so-called closed sport forms such
as throwing and jumping disciplines in track and field or apparatus
gymnastics. Comprehensive biomechanical movement description of open
sports taking place in large, open air areas are objects of neglect now as
before.

The measurement-technical expense of descriptive biomechanical movement analyses is very high insofar as a great demand must be placed on measurement accuracy; also measurement sensor influence on the movement sequence must be no more than very slight. As the analysis of complex movement techniques generally cannot take place in a laboratory but must occur rather under field conditions, this increases demands on diagnostic instruments to include mobility and field hardiness. How expensive the investigational equipment is will be shown here using an example conducted by the Institute of Sport Sciences at the University of Salzburg

Biomechanical description and analysis of the V technique in ski jumping (SCHWAMEDER/MÜLLER 1995).
The investigation was conducted using kinematic and dynamic measurement systems. Synchronized taping by two video cameras was used for determining the three dimensional location coordinates of selected reference points. This involved the video analysis system by the Peak company including an image processing and evaluation program as well as an auxiliary program for handling camera panning and tilting as well as focus-length adjustable cameras by DRENK (1994). The use of this auxiliary program presupposes a fixed pass point system which was installed on the investigational jumping hill in the area of motion. Black and white-dyed tennis balls mounted on steel cable at intervals of approximately a meter served as pass points, and both cameras were geodetically surveyed.

Force measurements were accomplished with help of the Emed System, manufactured by Novel, consisting of two pressure measuring soles (each with 85 capacitive pressure recorders at 40 Hz) and a control and memory unit.

The video recordings were manually digitized through a very time-intensive procedure. For evaluation of dynamic data, we layed a 55 x 40 matrix over the 170 sensors of both soles and determined the force values in each matrix field by means of an interpolation procedure. 8 members of the Austrian National Team stood ready as test subjects. Error estimation produced satisfactory results not only for kinematic, but also with dynamic characteristics. Using the calculated kinematic and dynamic characteristics, the investigated ski jump technique was first characterized and subsequently analyzed using statistical methods. An example of results is provided below:

Depicted in Fig. 7 are the mean and standard deviation course of the measured relative forces of 22 jumps. The motion phases are clearly recognizable: approach in the straight segment and in the transitional arc, launch, transitional phase, flight, landing preparation and landing.

F [%BW]

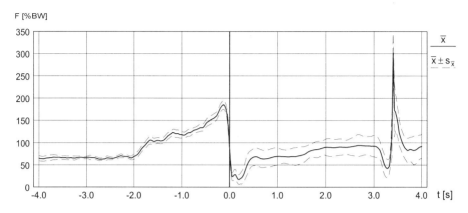

Fig. 7.   Force-time curve of relative total forces (time t = 0: Launch).

On average, 2 s before takeoff jumpers transition into the transitional arc whereby ground reaction forces due to centrifugal force occuring there significantly increase. Until departure from the transitional arc, the ground reaction forces increase to ca. 160% of body weight. The variations in the mean value and greater dispersion allow one to conclude that the transitional arc phase concerns a very sensitive phase of the run. Although the centrifugal force through entry into the flat segment of the jump table go to zero (t = -0.26 s), the ground reaction forces further increase, as conditioned by the take-off motion, reaching a maximum mean of 183 (+/- 8) % of body weight at = -0,136 s.

3.1.3 Profiles of sport-specific motor abilities
Given that a tightly scheduled, comprehensive competitive program has developed in elite sport, less and less time is available for conditioning training. Thus, the greatest efficiency via the best possible quality in training is of importance. Such training quality can be guaranteed only if sport-specific conditional variables of influence are very exactly known, testing procedures for checking them are ready at hand, and norm values for estimating the checked performance levels are available.
    In the context of a multi-year collaboration with the Austrian Tennis Federation, it was possible to produce a sport motor norm profile for tennis players ranging from age 10 to age 30 (MÜLLER et al. 1998; MÜLLER 1989). The investigational method employed comprised the following steps:

• Hypothetical selection of performance-related motor abilities
• Examination of the chosen abilities' relevance to performance

- Performance factor analysis - related tests
- Specific test battery including norm profiles and norm tables

Fig. 8 shows the motor performance level in the past two years of the No. 1 ranked ATP player beginning with 1996.

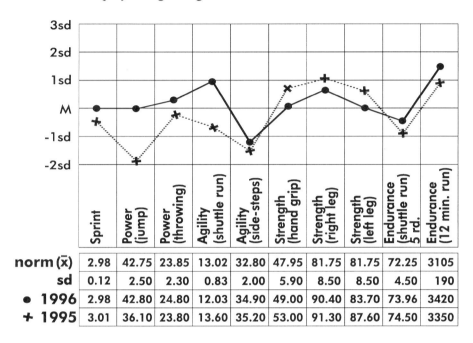

	Sprint	Power (jump)	Power (throwing)	Agility (shuttle run)	Agility (side-steps)	Strength (hand grip)	Strength (right leg)	Strength (left leg)	Endurance (shuttle run) 5 rd.	Endurance (12 min. run)
norm (x̄)	2.98	42.75	23.85	13.02	32.80	47.95	81.75	81.75	72.25	3105
sd	0.12	2.50	2.30	0.83	2.00	5.90	8.50	8.50	4.50	190
● 1996	2.98	42.80	24.80	12.03	34.90	49.00	90.40	83.70	73.96	3420
+ 1995	3.01	36.10	23.80	13.60	35.20	53.00	91.30	87.60	74.50	3350

Fig. 8.   The motor performance level of a top class ATP tennis player

3.2 Tests for checking the current, sport-specific level of performance

The quality of individual tests for checking a sport's performance-determining characteristics is very significant, as was mentioned at the outset. Above all, the chief criteria of validity, reliability and objectivity must be secured in high degree. This means, on the one hand, that tests must be very sport-specific and, on the other, exhibit very high measurement accuracy. Even when these demands appear obvious, one can point out that in the past valuable training time was all too often wasted by the use of unsuitable test procedures. In many cases tests which simply happened to be available were used in numerous, very differently structured sports without checking whether the respective sport's performance variables of influence were actually being measured.

The interpretation of such test results which arise under such conditions can lead to seriously false conclusions and thereby cause significant impairment of the training process.

The frequently-used endurance diagnostic for game sports can be cited as an example of this. For the most part, continuous endurance runs over 2,000 or 9,000 m and various 'line runs' with and without the ball have been used for checking general aerobic endurance. The preferred sports-medical test (spiroergometry; determining aerobic and/or anaerobic threshold) address different cardiopulmonary and metabolic parameters, yet concentrate on general aerobic or anaerobic capacity in the form of various laboratory and field tests. The greatest percentage of these tests is derived from typical endurance sports with nearly constant, cyclical load demands, for example from long distance running. An attempt to simulate the game sport-specific endurance loading structure, which can be characterized as intermittent (BANGSBO 1994) or acyclical (ZINTL 1994), is seldom.

An example of a game sport-specific endurance test was developed specifically for soccer by MÜLLER et al. (1992). In this test, imitation of the load structure diagnosed with help of a computer supported game analysis system (cf. Cap. 3.1.1.) was attempted. A 205 m running course depicted in Fig. 9 was constructed. This was negotiated 8 times per test subject. The running time per round was 78 seconds; the total time was 10:08 minutes. The course consisted of various soccer-specific movement tasks which were to be accomplished by the runner with like intensity. The running velocity is pregiven via an audio tape on which the seconds between the respective positions are counted down to zero.

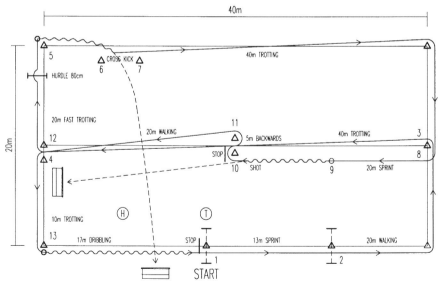

Fig. 9.   Running course for soccer-specific endurance.

Measured are the pulse rate both during and until 2 minutes after loading and the blood lactate concentration 1 minute after loading. The most predictive criterion variable is the lactate concentration 1 minute following loading. The validity of the test was conducted using the extreme group method (13 to 15 players each of the 1st, 2nd and 3rd Austrian divisions). The mean value differences between the players of the first division and the second and third divisions were respectively significant. The test/retest reliability check procedure resulted in correlation coefficients between 0.86 und 0.90, by which the test can be designated highly reliable.

3.3 Development of specific training devices

The necessity of using highly specific means of training applies chiefly to so-called seasonal sports such as Alpine ski racing. Alpine ski racing is one of those sports which make high demands on technical and physical abilities. This is made even more difficult by the fact that technique-specific training can be performed only on snow. Because snow-training in summer is very problematic due to organizational and financial reasons, technique-specific training is of high importance. In a further study, we have attempted developing training devices which make the performance of slalom-specific simulation exercises possible. These exercises should very closely approach the kinetic and kinematic structure of slalom technique. As a basis for the development of ski-racing specific simulation exercises, a detailed three dimensional kinematic and kinetic analysis of modern slalom technique was necessary. Members of the Austrian national teams served as test persons.

As an example Fig. 10 shows the ground reaction forces of the outer and inner leg, the inward leaning and the backwards leaning angle of a racer during a left and right turn. In the second part of this study various training devices were developed based on knowledge gained from the slalom analysis results. The greatest agreement in movement structures from competitive technique and training exercise can be achieved with the electronically controlled 'Ski Power Simulator'. Validity tests using the same measurement methods as for technical analysis on the slope delivered very satisfactory values both for dynamic and kinematic characteristics.

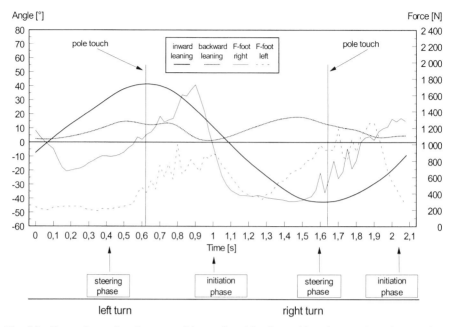

Fig. 10. Ground reaction forces and inward and backward leaning angles of a top class
skier during two slalom turns.

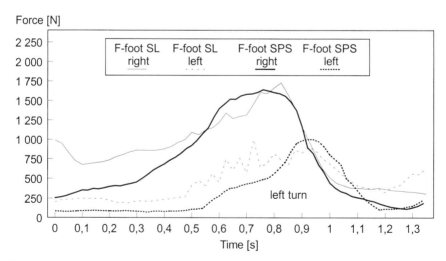

Fig. 11. Ground reaction forces of a top class skier during a slalom turn and during a
slalom imitation exercise on the Ski Power Simulator.

Fig. 11 compares ground reaction forces of a top class skier during a slalom turn with those of a slalom imitation exercise on the Ski Power Simulator. This example indicates the similarity of kinetic structure of the simulation exercise with the slalom performance on the slope.

3.4   Rapid turn around information systems for directing technique and conditioning

Numerous investigations in the area of motor learning and technical training have indicated in concert that suitable feedback systems can significantly contribute to shortening acquisition time (BARTLETT 1997; ROCKMANN-RÜGER 1991, DAUGS et al. 1989) according to the principle of „objectively supplementing rapid and immediate information" formulated by FARFEL (1977). These systems, on the one hand, should measure as exactly as possible the characteristics which are to be improved in training and, on the other, make the measurement results available to the athlete in an easily understandable form and within the most effective 'Prae-KR Interval' of 10 to 60 seconds.

Modern technical and conditioning training for many types of sport presently occurs in computer supported laboratories in which sport-specific competitive simulations can be conducted (PERL et al. 1997). Above all for so-called closed sports, for which competitive venues are standardized to a high degree, so-called „measurement training areas" are described in the literature (apparatus gymnastics: KNOLL 1996; KRUG et al. 1996; javelin: ADAMCZEWSKI 1995; wrestling: TÜNNEMANN/FREYER 1995).

In the contribution by Krug and Martin in this volume, measurement stations at the Institute for Applied Training Science in Leipzig are introduced in detail.

In collaboration with the Austrian Marksmanship Federation, a laboratory training area for rifle and pistol marksmanship was established at the Institute of Sport Sciences of the University of Salzburg. During training one can here measure the course of the shooter's center of gravity, heart and breath rate as well as the shooters trigger force brought to bear on the trigger and simultaneously displayed on a screen. Additionally, the aiming motion of the weapon is recorded using a laser measuring system (Fig. 12). All measurement data can be simultaneously followed on the screen or, respectively, interpreted together with the athlete directly after the shot.

Fig. 12. Laboratory measurement station for marksmanship at the Institute for Sport
Sciences in Salzburg.

4 Literature

ADAMCZEWSKI, H. (1995). Ergebnisse sportspezifischer Untersuchungen
auf dem Meßplatz Speerwurf. In Schriftenreihe zur angewandten
Trainingswissenschaft, 2 (3), 90-104.

BALLREICH, R. (1996). Untersuchungsziele des Sports. In BALLREICH,
R., BAUMANN, W. (Hrsg.). Grundlagen der Biomechanik des Sports
(S.13-53). Stuttgart: Enke.

BANGSBO, J. (1994). Energy demands in competitive soccer. In Journal
of Sports Sciences, 12, 5-12.

BARTLETT, R.M. (1997). Current issues in the mechanics of athletic
activities. A position paper. In J. Biomechanics, 30 (5), 447-486.

BERNWICK, U., MÜLLER, E. (1995). Computergestützte Spielanalyse im
Spitzentennis. In Leistungssport, 25 (3), 11-14.

BERNWICK, U., MÜLLER, E. (1995). Aktuelle Spielanalysen im
internationalen Spitzentennis der Herren. In Leistungssport, 25 (4), 23-
27

BEST, R.J., BARTLETT, R.M., SAWYER, R.A. (1995). Optimal Javelin Release. In Journal of applied Biomechanics, 11, 371-394.

BOIKO, V. V. (1989). Die gezielte Entwicklung der Bewegungsfähigkeiten des Menschen. Moskau 1987, partly translated in: TSCHIENE, P. Die neue Theorie des Training's und ihre Interpretation für das Nachwuchstraining. In: Leistungssport, 1, 11 - 17.

DAUGS, R., BLISCHKE, K., OLIVIER, N., MARSCHALL, F. (1989). Beiträge zum visuomotorischen Lernen, Schorndorf: Hofmann.

DJATSCHKOW, W. M. (1977). Die Steuerung und Optimierung des Trainingsprozesses. Berlin: Bartels & Wernitz KG.

FARFEL, W.S. (1977). Bewegungssteuerung im Sport, Berlin: SportVerlag

FERRAUTI, A., WEBER, K. (1991). Systematische Videoanalyse des Wimbledon-Finales 1990 zwischen Edberg und Becker. In Leistungssport, 21 (2), 32-35.

FRÖHNER, B. (1995). Aktuelle Computer- und Videotechnologie zur systematischen Untersuchung des technisch-taktischen Handelns im Volleyball aus individueller und mannschaftstaktischer Sicht. In Leistungssport, 25 (3), 4-10.

HILDEBRAND, F., WAGNER, K. (1997). Technologische Entwicklungen und ihre Einflüsse auf die Leistungsentwicklung, Trainingssteuerung und Wettkampfführung. In Zeitschrift für Angewandte Trainingswissenschaft, 4 (1), 6-25.

KNOLL, K., (1995). Ingenieur- und meßtechnische Aspekte zur Objektivierung der Sporttechnik mit Meßplätzen im Kunstturnen. In Schriftenreihe zur angewandten Trainingswissenschaft, 2 (3), 57-78.

KRUG, J., HEILFORT, U., ZINNER, J. (1996). Digitales Video- und Signalverarbeitungssystem - DIGVIS. In Leistungssport, 26 (1), 13-16.

LOY, R. (1995). Systematische Spielbeobachtung im Fußball. In Leistungssport, 25 (3), 15-20.

LAMES, M. (1991). Leistungsdiagnostik durch Computersimulation. Ein Beitrag zur Theorie der Sportspiele am Beispiel Tennis. Bd. 17 der Beiträge zur Sportwissenschaft. Frankfurt am Main: Harri Deutsch.

LAMES, M. (1994). Systematische Spielbeobachtung. Münster: Philippka.

MÜLLER, E. (1989). Sportmotorische Testverfahren zur Talentauswahl im Tennis. In Leistungssport, 19 (2), 5-9.

MÜLLER, E., WACHTER, E. (1989). Trainingsmethoden zur Verbesserung der speziellen Sprungkraft von Skispringern. In Spectrum der Sportwissenschaften, 1 (1), 47-71.

MÜLLER, E. (1992). Leistungsdiagnostik - Theorie und Wirklichkeit. In BERNHARD, G., KLAUTZER G. (Hrsg.). Training und Wettkampf -

Arbeitsberichte des Symposiums „Sport - Sinn und Wahn" (S. 67-80), Graz: Eigenverlag.

MÜLLER, E., LORENZ, H. (1996). Computergestütztes Spielanalysesystem im Spitzenfußball, 26 (1), 59-62.

MÜLLER, E., BENKO, U., RASCHNER, C., SCHWAMEDER, H. (1998). Specific Fitness Training and Testing in Competitive Sports. In Medicine and Science in Sports and Exercise, in press.

NIGG, B.M. (1993). Sports science in the twenty-first century. In: Journal of Sports Sciences, 11, 342-347.

PERL, J., LAMES, M., MIETHLING, W.-D. (Hrsg.). (1997). Informatik im Sport. Ein Handbuch. Bd. 117 der Beiträge zur Lehre und Forschung im Sport. Schorndorf: Hofmann.

RASCHNER, C. (1997). Kinematische und dynamische Technikanalyse im Slalom als Grundlage für die Entwicklung skispezifischer Krafttrainingsgeräte und Krafttrainingsmethoden, Diss., Universität Salzburg

RASCHNER, C., MÜLLER, E., SCHWAMEDER, H. (1997). Kinematic and kinetic analysis of slalom turns as a basis for the development of specific training methods to improve strength and endurance. In MÜLLER, E., SCHWAMEDER, H., KORNEXL, E., RASCHNER, C. (Hrsg.). Science and Skiing (S. 251-261). London FN Spon.

REILLY, T., CLARYS, J., STIBBE, A. (Hrsg.). (1993). Science and Football II. London: FN Spon.

ROCKMANN-R‹GER, U., (1991). Zur Gestaltung von Übungsprozessen beim Erlernen von Bewegungstechniken, Frankfurt am Main: Deutsch.

SCHWAMEDER, H., MÜLLER, E. (1995). Biomechanische Beschreibung und Analyse der V-Technik im Skispringen. In Spectrum der Sportwissenschaften, 7 (1), 5-36.

SIFF, M.C., VERKHOSHANSKY, Y. V. (1996). Supertraining. Special Strength Training for Sporting Excellence, Pittsburgh: Sports Support Syndicate.

TÜNNEMANN, H., FREYER, K. (1995). Diagnostik und Training technikorientierter Kraftfähigkeiten mittels ringkampfspezifischer Bewegungssimulatoren. In Schriftenreihe zur angewandten Trainingswissenschaft, 2 (3), 105-121.

WERCHOSHANSKI, J.W. (1988). Effektiv Trainieren, Berlin: Sport Verlag

YEADON, M.R., ATHA, J., HALES, F. D. (1990). The simulation of aerial movement. Part IV: a computer simulation model. In Journal of Biomechanics, 23, 58-89.

YEADON, M.R., CHALLIS, J.H. (1994). The future of performance-related sports biomechanics research. In Journal of Sports Sciences, 12, 3-32.

ZATSIORSKY, V. M. (1996). Krafttraining - Wissenschaft und Praxis. Aachen: Meyer & Meyer.

ZIMMERMANN, B. (1995). Computergestützte Wettkampfanalyse zur unmittelbaren Spielsteuerung im Volleyball. In Zeitschrift für angewandte Trainingswissenschaft, 2 (2), 105-121

ZINTL, F. (1994). Ausdauertraining, München: BLV.

2
THE CONTRIBUTION OF SPORTS MEDICINE TO TRAINING EFFICIENCY AND PERFORMANCE CAPACITY OPTIMIZATION IN HIGH-PERFORMANCE SPORT

N. BACHL
Austria

Keywords: aptitude diagnosis, Austria, health stabilization, performance diagnosis, rehabilitation, resources, sports medicine.

A training program tailored to adaptive laws should provide maximum enhancement of an athlete's performance. Since several factors determine a human being's maximum psycho-physical performance, this process needs to be supported through application of several scientific disciplines. Sports medicine is a discipline of special significance in this context. On the one hand, sports medicine is responsible for ensuring stable health as a prerequisite for optimal training. On the other, based on the outcome of physiological and biological research, sports medicine can provide new inputs for controlling the training process and enhancing athletic performance. Throughout the entire range of sport, i.e. from the child who engages in occasional games to high-performance athletes, particular medical disciplines and specialties vary in degree of importance, depending on the topic of study or the question being investigated. Research of this nature is focused on general clinical, endocrinological, immunological and molecular biological findings as well as on questions concerning the apparatus of posture and locomotion (the musculoskeletal system). On these foundations, performance physiology and molecular biology occupy a central role in controlling and monitoring the training process as well as in handling adaptive processes which are a result of these.

The purpose of the following five-point stratification is to elucidate ways in which sports medicine can aid performance optimization in competitive sports in general and delineate these aspects in the Austrian context:

1. Content-related aspects
2. Structural and organizational conditions
3. Personnel
4. Financial resources
5. Free space

1 Content-related aspects

In accordance with organismic systems and their functions as defined by Neumann and Schüller in 1989, a distinction can be made between general and local adaptations induced by training. General adaptive reactions primarily concern autonomic processes - especially central-somatic, neural and humoral adjustment processes - whose biological value lies in the fact that they ensure local adjustment as well as reactions related to local adjustment. The latter are defined as processes triggered by specific stimuli. These processes trigger simultaneously and take place at the site of causation. Some of these processes are auto-regulative while others are coupled back with general adaptation (Neumann, Schüller, 1989). Consequently, the purpose of optimizing performance is to support local and general adaptation processes in such a manner that the formation of specific changes within system complexes is augmented.

System complexes within the organism

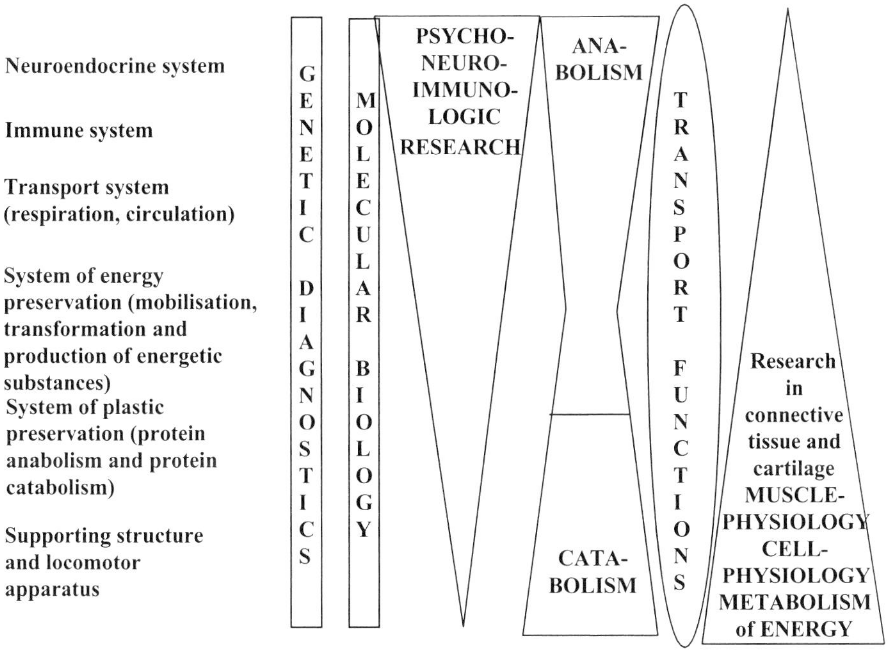

Fig. 1.   System complexes within the organism.

Keeping in mind the interaction between the stress and strain to which an athlete is subjected, the aim of such a training program is to achieve specifically those adaptations which constitute the structural requirements of a specific kind of sport, which are to be achieved by a systematized training process. In cooperation with other sports science sub-specialties, sports medicine is faced with the following task in the area of scientific research and its practical application:

1.1 Health stabilization

The results of examinations described in the following constitute the criteria for health stabilization. These examinations are performed both under resting and stress conditions. Differential diagnostic criteria are the regulative changes at sub-maximal and maximal stress in view of the achievable or achieved level of adaptation.

1.1.1 Internal and orthopedic clinical questions; if necessary all other clinical specialties as well as traumatological and rehabilitative measures
1.1.2 Endocrinological, gynecological and andrological questions
1.1.3 Psycho-neuroimmunological questions
1.1.4 Nutrition and substitution

1.2 Aptitude diagnosis

Aptitude Diagnosis

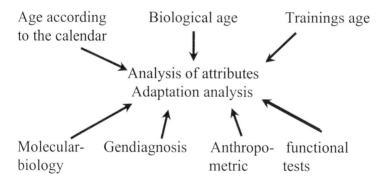

Fig. 2.   Aspects of aptitude diagnosis.

The results of molecular biology and genetic research have demonstrated the following: First, attributes that determine the performance of a human being are multilocular in the human genome. Second, a distinction must be made between a specific performance attribute per se and its range of adaptation (trainability). This could mean, for instance, that a higher maximal intake of oxygen alone is no absolute criterion of a future international champion in disciplines associated with tenacity (staying power). This would be indicative only if this attribute has the potential of being increased to an unusually high extent through training. In any case, the results of current studies, especially the inheritance and gene/athlete study, remain to be seen. Along with classical examination procedures such as anthropometry, sports medical tests etc., the findings of molecular biology (e.g. myosin heavy-chain analyses) and results of genetic diagnostic studies must be interpreted in close cooperation with training sciences, because alterations in a particular attribute that is a requirement of a particular kind of sport depend upon training stresses that are defined in terms of time and content.

1.3 Performance diagnosis – Structural diagnosis

Within the framework of the sports medical examination, the purpose of performance and structure diagnosis is defined as follows. On the one hand, these forms of diagnosis provide a structural analysis for maximum performance and, on the other, they determine the current status such that current values can be compared with target values. Training measures are decided upon based on this comparison.

These examinations are based on the stress-strain concept defined by PANSOLD.

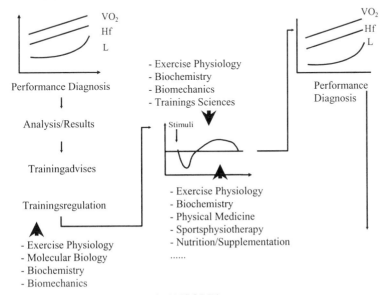

Fig.3. Stress-strain concept (PANSOLD).

In all examinations related to performance diagnosis, whether they concern semi-specific laboratory studies or specific field studies, the challenge for sports medicine and performance physiology in the near future will be to physically document the overall structure and the sectional structures of stress relating to each kind of sport by the use of modern technology. This incorporates the application of micro-electronic elements, the use of suitable hardware and software and modern methods of telemetric data transfer and data storage. This documentation should be done carefully so that the strain imposed by each kind of sport on biological systems in terms of local and general adaptation, is registered as accurately as possible. For this purpose, micro-analytical and semi-invasive or non-invasive procedures must be used more extensively in order to document the course of regulatory and adaptive processes e.g. by means of time series analyses. While changes relating to molecular biology, especially those taking place in the contractile proteins of skeletal muscles, have to be obtained by invasive procedures, several metabolic parameters can be documented by non-invasive techniques which, together with suitable statistical analyses, will make it possible to carry out time series studies.

1.4 Sports medical care

Control of stress and regeneration is the basis of local and general adaptation mechanisms. Increasing efficiency in terms of an optimum "cost-utility ratio" (dose-response relationship) can be achieved if maximum levels of training stress are integrated into a single day or into one or more microcycles in accordance with the respective training phase. This integration should be such that all possible regenerative measures are applied to produce a regenerated and efficient organism. The following aspects may be regarded as the main focus of sports medical care:

Health stabilization

- Controlling stress and regeneration on the basis of what is known about stress-strain reactions
- Supporting the dynamics of regenerative processes, especially by implementing physical measures and paying special attention to "connective tissue regeneration"
- Sports medical care in training camps, in the period preceding competition as well as during competition.
- Care under special environmental conditions, especially altitudes, temperature and humidity

- Nutrition, substitution
- Sport orthopedics – sport traumatologic care
- Rehabilitation

The findings obtained from the examination techniques detailed in the chapter on aptitude and performance diagnosis are also a part of sports medical care. It should be mentioned that a discussion of these measures will have to include modern endocrinologic and genetic diagnosis along with addressing the problem of increasing efficiency by means of drugs and methods that are prohibited by or not even known to medical commissions, the IOC and other professional associations.

While the majority of sports medical research, whether basic or applied, is carried out within the specialties by the respective specialists, sports medical care is the domain of "specialists in sports medicine". Today, there are several countries in Europe where the specialist for sports medicine is a recognized entity. The curriculum of this specialty includes internal medicine, orthopedics, traumatology, physical medicine and rehabilitation, physiology, biology, training sciences, psychology and several others. Within various committees, the European Society of Sports medicine is now making serious efforts to establish sports medicine (and specialists in sports medicine) as a separate specialty within the European Union.

2 Structural and organizational conditions

In relation to the sports medical requirements mentioned in chapter 1, the following subjects may be defined as the focus of basic and applied research in the near future:

- Energy metabolism: Biopsy, MRI, simulation, energy mobilization etc
- Muscle physiology: Expression forms of MHC, IGF, MGF, etc.
- Membrane function
- Metabolic markers
- Anabolism – catabolism
- Transport function
- Connective tissue and cartilage research
- Neurology, endocrinology and immunology research
- Genetic research: Attributes, adaptation, role-playing control mechanisms

In light of these focal points, sports medical and scientific activities of

Austrian research scientists need assume their rightful place in the international setting. Although a number of positive approaches have been attempted, especially in sports medical care and in applied research (in the course of training sportsmen), there is a regrettable deficiency of apparatuses as well as personnel and financial resources in the field of basic research. This deficit will make it difficult to support competitive sports in the coming years. Notwithstanding several promises made by competent authorities and ministries, it must be mentioned that systematized basic research in the above mentioned areas is not feasible or only marginally feasible today in Austria. Efforts in basic research and applied research are mostly single initiatives from individuals, university departments or teaching institutions. Because of these restrictions, these efforts do not attain the aggregate common in the international setting. It should be remembered that this aggregate is necessary to adequately support high-performance sports. One example of this phenomenon is the output in scientific research by way of lectures at international meetings.

33rd German Sport Medical Congress
Paderborn, 1993

Ratio of Contributions of Austrian Scientists for special topics in the Field of Sports Medicine

Exercise Physiology	60/3
The Immune System, Hematology	14/0
Molecular Biology	25/0
Endocrinology	
Orthopedics and Sportstraumatology	39/0
Osteoporosis	18/1

34th German Sport Medical Congress
Saarbrücken, 1995

Ratio of Contributions of Austrian Scientists for special topics in the Field of Sports Medicine

Internal Medicine	38/3
Exercise Physiology	43/2
Endocrinology	30/0
The Immune System, Hematology, Molecular Biology	20/0
Orthopedics and Sportstraumatology	44/1

35th German Sport Medical Congress
Tübingen, 1997

Ratio of Contributions of Austrian Scientists for special topics in the Field of Sports Medicine

Cardiac Rehabilitation	48/0
Exercise Physiology	51/5
The Immune System, hematology, Molecular Biology	32/1
Endocrinology, Metabolism	23/1
Sportsorthopedics-Sportstraumatology	92/3

2nd Annual Congress of the European College of Sports Science - Sports Science in a Changing World of Sports
Copenhagen, 1997

Ratio of Contributions of Austrian Scientists for special topics in the Field of Sports Medicine

The Immune System and Exercise	4/0
Lab Tests, Field Tests	8/1
Muscle Physiology	9/0
Muscle Energetics	8/0
Cardio Vascular Response to Exercise	8/0
Respiratory Response during Exercise	7/1

33rd International Congress of Physiological Science
St. Petersburg, 1997

Ratio of Contributions of Austrian Scientists for special topics in the Field of Sports Medicine

Oxydant Regulation of Cellular Functions	5/0
Muslce Fibre Composition, Effects of Performance	5/0
Muscle Physiology in Space	8/1
Gas Exchange and Pulmonary Circulation	5/0
Integrative Physiology and Evolutionary Design of Muscular System	5/0
Oxygen, Antioxidants and Exercise	5/0
Respiration in Extreme Environment	6/0
Maximal Performance in Locomotion	6/0

Steroid Receptors	5/0
Physiological Adaptation of Muscle to Use	8/0
Neuroimmunology	6/0

Since basic research in performance physiology and all specialties and disciplines allied to it have had a fruitful effect on clinical medicine, it may be hoped that research in performance medicine in Austria will be given due importance and that more funds, personnel and technology will be made available by the competent public authorities, as is already the case in many other European and non-European countries. This will have to be preceded by a change in structural and organizational conditions in Austria. In particular, it will be necessary to delineate the limits of competence (at present sport, promotion of sports and the promotion of scientific research in sport is controlled by too many mutually dependent, overlapping or networked committees). Furthermore, the structure will have to include a research promotion office which will be entrusted with the task of defining research topics and research projects and assigning these to the respective university institutes, departments and special hospitals. One of the prerequisites of this anticipatory development is that the public and its representatives must make an explicit commitment to sport, the promotion of sports and promotion of scientific work, also in terms of innovative spin-offs, prevention and rehabilitation. These measures to promote research must be complemented by special centers for specific kinds of sport, a medical commission created in accordance with professional criteria within the IOC, and allocation of funds for applying the results of sports medical research as well as adequate sports medical care.

3 Personnel

At first glance the number of active sports medical physicians in Austria appears sufficient for carrying out the task delineated above (Table). However, the (not entirely complete) list of sports medical specialists in various institutions shows that, compared to what is required, the personnel actually available for this task is very limited. This is especially true for internal medicine, performance physiology, endocrinology, immunology and meta-bolic research. Out-patient departments of traumatology and orthopedics appear to be well staffed with physicians and able to offer more compre-hensive care. However, even for these specialties there exist large gaps in basic research (connective tissue research, cartilage research etc.).

Personal Resources

Members of the Austrian Federation of Sports Medicine	752
Physicians with the Austrian Sport Medical Diplom	656

Specialisation
Exercise Physiology	4

Additional Specialisation (Subspecialisation)
Sportstraumatology	83
Internal Sportsmedicine	19
Physikal Sportsmedicine	11
Sportsorthopedics	26

Personal Resources

Institution	physicians	MTA/F	Bio	S
Clinic of University Internal Medicine - AKH Wien	2 VB	-/2 VB		
IMSB	1 VB	1 VB/	1	
Clinic of University Children Surgery Graz	1 VB	1 TZ		1 VB
Institute for Sportsmedicine of Kärnten, Klagenfurt	1 VB, 1 TZ	2 VB/-		
Institute for Sportsmedicine Krems	2 VB			3 VB
Hospital Feldkirch/Institute f. Sportsmedicine	1 VB, 1 TZ			1 TZ
IfS Dept.Sportsphysiology Wien	4 VB	1 VB/-		2 TZ
Austrian Institute for Sportsmedicine, Wien	1 VB 5 TZ	2 VB		
Physiologisches Institut der Uni Graz	1 VB	1 TZ/-		2 TZ

VB=full employed, TZ=half employed; MTA=Medical Technical Assistent, S=others; B=biochemist;

Personal Resources

Institution	physicians	MTA/F	Bio	S
Institut für Sportmedizin, Innsbruck	5 VB	2 VB/-	1	3+
Hospital St. Johann/Inst. f. Sportsmedicine	2 1/2 VB	1 VB/-		2 VB
Institute for Sportmedicin des Landes Salzburg	2 VB 2 TZ			
Hanuschkrankenhaus Wien	8 VB *			3 VB
Unfallkrankenhaus Salzburg	4 VB *			1 VB
Landeskrankenhaus Salzburg	9 VB *			
Uniklinik Graz Unfallchirurgie	2-3 VB *			2 VB
Unfallkrankenhaus Graz	2 VB *			
LKH Stolzalpe	2 VB *			
Uniklinik f. Unfallchirurgie Innsbruck (1/Woche Sportambulance)	4 VB *			

* abwechselnd im Ambulanzbetrieb

4 Financial resources

In Austria a small part of sports medical examination costs are refunded. Specific sportsmen are nominated by sport organizations and the costs of various examinations are reimbursed in accordance with a low scale of rates (Table). Contrary to the requirements of sports medical care, this system of reimbursement is based on a non-specific "watering can principle". It fails to fulfill international standard of sports medical care. In this area too, there is an urgent necessity to carefully consider nationally coordinated and applicable scales of rates for specific examinations related to specific kinds of sport. The rates should be such that the actual costs of examination are covered. Without going into the details of various special examinations, the following areas urgently need to be considered in addition to the existing ones: Special laboratory examinations (e.g. neuro-immunologic parameters, endocrinologic parameters), imaging procedures, a number of stress examinations in the laboratory and field at appropriate intervals during the course of training (there is a large deficiency in these areas as well as in molecular biologic and imaging procedures) and monitoring of physical regeneration. Since Austria is openly committed to high-performance sports and since international success in sports is evaluated as a positive enhancement of Austria's image, economy and tourism, care should be taken to ensure that the internationally applicable standards of sports medical research and care prevail in Austria.

Example: ELITE SPORTS CHECK

Financial Refundings:

Internal Check	öS 300,--
Ergometry with Lactate Analysis	öS 250,--
Spiroergometry with Lactate Analysis	öS 450,--
Orthopedic Check	öS 150,--

For ballsports for example handball, table tennis, 1 sportmedicial investigation per year (1 internal Check, 1 orthopedic check, 1 ergometry with lactate will be refunded)
For endurance sports for example cycling, mountainbiking, athletics, trake and field, orienteering (1 internal check and 1 orthopedic check and 2 spiroergometric investigations per year will be refunded)

5 Free space

The following quote is attributed to one of the presidents of the Max Plank Society:

"How much future a country has depends on its level of science and research. How good research is depends on the talent of research scientists and the genius of the best among them. However, how good research scientists can be and to what extent geniuses can evolve in that setting, depends on the structure in which they work, the resources available to them and the free space available to them when research starts to conflict with other values and interests. I would like to have a university that does not have to constantly defend before society its desire to consciously pursue basic research. The discussion as to whether theoretical or applied research should have priority is, in my opinion, superfluous. The indivisible and close interrelationship between basic research, technology and economy is long established. In fact, what makes basic research so fascinating is the fact that its future applications cannot be foreseen in the present time."

Much cannot be added to this statement. From time to time, one cannot refrain from thinking that in a country where cruelty to animals is discussed with greater emotion than child abuse, a misguided notion of pseudo-humanism often creates an atmosphere of hostility towards research. This atmosphere fosters irrational discussions on genetic technology and imposes drastic limitations on research, as a result of decisions made by ethics commissions. This should not be misinterpreted as a general criticism of prevailing or planned regulatory measures. However, it should be mentioned that some invasive procedures which could produce innovative findings in sports medicine, performance physiology, orthopedics and traumatology, are highly restricted in Austria.

These "highlights" are not only criticisms; they may also be regarded as points of departure or suggestions. They do not veil the existing structures or invalidate the positive efforts being made in several institutions and sport associations. As in a number of other fields, the degree of success achieved by individual initiatives, small projects and sponsors is remarkable. A further positive aspect is that, based on the example of a winter sport association, several summer sport associations are trying to implement long-term care programs in cooperation with institutions concerned with sports medicine and sports science.

Nevertheless, in summary it should be mentioned again that from the point of view of sports medicine, there should be a significant enhancement of personnel, funds and apparatuses, in basic research and its application, and in applied sports medicine, so that the sciences are able to achieve innovative research results which will contribute to the outstanding international performance of Austria's athletes.

3
SCIENCE - NO THANKS!
THESES AGAINST A FRUITLESS VENTURE

G. SCHUMACHER
Germany

Keywords: biomechanics, Germany, media, physiology, psychology, social interaction, trainer.

1 Introduction

The provocative opening formulation is intended to document the science-unfriendly attitude on the part of trainers encountered in actual practice. The tension-filled relationship between scientists and trainers is based on the doggedly complex mode of observation of the one and the interest in immediately applicable advice for the other. A tension with consequences!?

The following discussion from the standpoint of the trainer shall indicate those roll definitions which lead to a mutual blockade. The consciously exaggerated depiction and intentional provocation highlight some personal experiences from the sport of speed skating which turned out ultimately to be "stumbling blocks".

Initial thesis
Scientists and trainers must be clear about their common role in service of the success of the athlete and also desire to fulfill this role. If each would entertain thinking into the work world and language of the respective partner, then the statement of trainers could clearly be: Science - yes gladly!

My own experience shows that research initiatives from the scientific ivory tower rarely are crowned with success as problem solutions in the competitive event. As a basis for the manner of preceding, here the Eisenhower principle solely holds.

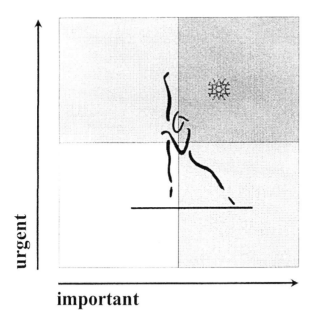

important

Examples from scientific disciplines

Psychology ('Questionnaires instead of answers')
If the success of the athlete is the measure of all efforts, then kilometer-long questionnaires contribute rather little to this goal. Athletes and trainers already have enough questions for themselves. What is expected of a psychologist is that he or she observes, listens, analyzes and offers competent help. One of the essential tasks in which psychologists can bring an indispensable contribution to the success of the team is social competence - not in the sense of the fireman who conjures up current problem solutions but rather as a guiding strategist who in the area of misdevelopment initially recognizes, prevents, or at least provides help in correction - the psychologist is to be understood in this role.

The possible interpersonal relationship fields for the main actors in sport are given in Table 1.

Table 1. Social interaction fields.

	Participants	**Trainer**	**Club**
Persons	Participants	Trainer	Functionaries
	Trainer	Participants	Participants, Trainers
	Functionaries	Functionaries	Advisors
	Advisers	Advisers	Family/Friends/Area
	Family/Friends/Area	Family/Friends/Area	
Institutions	Club	Club	Club
	Association	Association	Association
	Sport Assistance	Sport Assistance	Sport Assistance
	BW/BGS/Employer/	BW/BGS/Employer/	BW/BGS/Employer/
	University	University	University
	Club Sponsors	Club Sponsors	Club Sponsors
	Individual Sponsors	Individual sponsors	Individual Sponsors
	Ministry	Ministry	Ministry
	Media	Media	Media

Two important practical solution initiatives for development of social competency are:

- an attempt to first understand the conversation partners;
- to foster understanding by supplying the right word at the right moment in the right manner.

Physiology ('...more boldness with soft data')
Medical measuring technology indeed allows a reading of lactate concentration to two decimal places, yet -

- do these two decimal places help direct training?
- is this not a fruitless venture?
- isn't the athlete's subjective lactate perception not the more important guiding parameter which the investigations need to serve?

Specifically, the stated lactate perception of the athlete is mystified everywhere and considered important; but this concept is applied only seldomly. Personal experience also shows here that top athletes are able to estimate their physiological demand with great precision. Collaboration with science should succeed in contributing to the development of this capability and concentrate less on amassed data sets.

Praxis has additionally shown that the supposedly hard data and spot which the trainer completes using lap splits later prove to be false estimations. Athletes guided by subjective impressions contradict these benchmarks - and they are right!

Athletes must be brought alongside for collaboration and thought; they act as measuring instruments and chronometers. Through this various perceptions will be registered in a functioning communicative context and not lead to pitfalls.

Open, informed, collaborating athletes are a challenge for trainers and athletes. Mutual acceptance, the struggle for solutions and encountering argument effects a continuously newly motivated team spirit.

Biomechanics ("...impulse transmission instead of data graveyard")

Biomechanics, even more so than medicine, runs the risk of becoming a "data graveyard" full of numbers, data and facts. Speed skaters in wind tunnel movement training or also other investigations here offer innumerable opportunities for this. Yet, of what use are these indeed so comprehensive and finely diced evaluations if they first come out punctually after the last competition of the season - or if central points disappear in a "verbal fog" of formulae, technical concepts and consequences?

For the participants, the sentence "Up with your behind!" is more profitable than biomechanically correct formulations such as "attempt to structure the start such that blade momentum is directed to the body's center of gravity wherewith the body mass is accelerated as much as possible in the running line, achieving a constant speed with high power momentum values" - this is a question of communication and didactics which unfortunately are not always observed in biomechanics.

Case Example 1

Already in 1988, wind tunnel tests settled a matter which we journalists actively assisted from idea to the search for sponsors, without reporting about it in the foreground.

Speeds achieved in the 5000m race (45-48 km/h) are sufficient to allow wind resistance to become a performance-influencing variable. The questions thus were directed towards differently constructed racing suits and their aerodynamic characteristics as well as effects on speed (cf. Fig. 2).

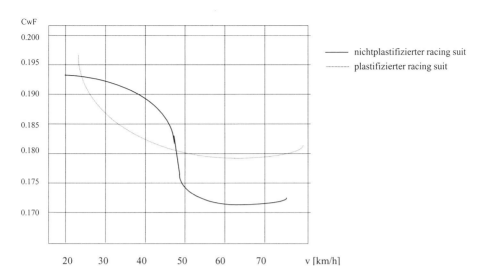

Fig. 2.   CwF course in dependence upon traveling velocity for two different racing suits; particularly of interest is the range of speed between 40 and 50 km/h.

The anthropometrically defined crouch of the Austrian top athlete M.H. effects from an aerodynamic point of view a disadvantage of 0.81m per 10s (ca. 2.43m per lap). The result from the measurements in the wind tunnel was a foam piece on the neck which positively influenced the air flow. This change in the body profile of the racer was banned following the Olympic Games by the World Federation.

Case Example 2
The Olympic victory of Olaf Zinke can be cited as a further example in which science was involved in the development of a creative alternative. Colleagues at the IAT in Leipzig calculated for him very promising speed parameters in the final segment of the 500m sprint. A top calculation was produced for the 1000m race and discussed with the trainer. Behavioral guidelines concerning entering curves were discussed with the trainer and the trainer communicated a feeling of confidence to the athlete that in the 1000m there were justified hopes for success.

The result: For the public a 'nobody' was the Olympic champion; in reality it was the man standing on the summit of a functioning team.

Media ("Popularity as Science")

Media and sponsoring are today their own science for which athletes need not only specialists who show ways to success but also to gain the insight that neither of these areas can be wished away out of sport.

Even when it is difficult to bring this into consonance with our traditional understanding of sport, now more than ever the expression holds, "a competition about which nothing is reported has never occurred."

The German Speed Skating Federation holds one to two times per year a media seminar outside the context of hectic competitive activity in order to extensively discuss developing rules for interacting with the media. Here is a personal thesis concerning the topic of "information training": "A bad answer not infrequently has something to do with a bad question!"

As delivering a respectively meaningful product to the public should be the goal of both journalists and athletes, nothing is more important than informed cooperation.

The financial aspect here plays a very important role and is an essential extrinsic motivational factor - and without the media there is no sponsoring. Thus in this many sided arena additional personnel are brought into play - specifically the manager. Some are an ideal complement in the advising team, some however produce an impression as if they were on the side of the other team. The measure of all things designated at the outset as social competence should once again be applied. Under this common denominator, all of the individual factors can be meaningfully integrated.

Speed skating has developed further and done much for a better effect on the public. Chattering belongs to this craft and proverbially the speed skaters have introduced the chattering ice skate.

Conclusion

Trainer and scientist- competition without battle: The complexity of sport demands that the trainer understand experts in the various respective specialties. Only when he speaks their language can he bring a filter into play by which he can reduce the multiplicity of expert suggestions down to essentials which at the close of the day benefit the athlete in competition.

A rivalry between the athlete's service providers would be counter-productive. The argument between "my data clearly show" and "but my experience says" will in the future also lie in the path of the athlete. Without personal vanities or ivory tower abstract modes of thought, however, trainers and scientists make a lustrous team.

4

SPECIFICS OF RESEARCH IN ELITE SPORT - EXAMPLES AND EXPERIENCES IN GERMANY

J. KRUG and D. MARTIN
Institute for Applied Training Science, University of Leipzig, Germany

Keywords: competition research, coordination, diving, figure skating, gymnastics, Germany, information systems, preparatory research, process accompanying training, wrestling.

1 Introduction

Elite sport is a special field in the complex spectrum of sport. In recent years elite sport was increasingly separated from other fields. It is therefore not surprising to see that new scientific methods and approaches were also developed. It is interesting that political conditions in several countries show the influence of structural and organizational elements in elite sport. This area of sports is therefore influenced by different general and specific elements.

For the present we should propose to define the term elite sport. We use this for athletes, "who by pertinent national authorities are recognized as participants, or having the potential to participate, in major sports events such as Olympic Games, World Championships and European Championships" (BOUCHOUT, 1993, pp. 174). At this high level of performance there are many topics for investigation and scientific advising for training.

After the discussion of some aspects from a theoretical scientific point of view we address organizational-structural particularities in Germany. Moreover, we rehearse our ideas for "process-accompanying training and competition research" (MARTIN et al., 1996) as a special research typology in elite sport.

2 Methodological approach

In recent years performance in most kinds and disciplines of a high performance competitive sport has increased. It seems to be the case that an end in performance development will not be reached. This growth is based on the continual improvement of training methods and training systems. The enhanced performance is connected with a higher load in the training. As elite sport leads one to the limits of human performance capacity, national sport systems create contexts typical of their nation for developing top performance. Within these contexts, the research subsystem has increasingly gained significance. In many countries scientifically oriented advising for training and competition is an important condition for the further development of performance. Simultaneously ethical and moral factors play a significant role in training and competition. The international trend towards the institutionalization of this research is interesting. Institutionalization is one of the criteria in the typology of a developing science. WILLIMCZIK (1985) discussed additional criteria for independent scientific disciplines using sport science as an example:

- independent field of subjects
- specific research methods
- systematics of knowledge
- level of institutionalization.

From a philosophy of science point of view the existence of paradigms (KUHN, 1962) is also very important. National particularities are an image of the respective research landscapes.

Areas of considerations for elite sport research could be, for example, sociological, organizational-theoretical, medical-biological, but also training-scientific. This paper has essentially a training-scientific orientation.

The type of research engaged in elite sport concerns a practice-oriented understanding of science. Characteristics include small groups and a high level of significance accorded to individual analyses and the articulation of individual results. Essential contents concern the effect analysis of training and of the trajectory of the performance profile for competition, as well as the avoidance of health risks, which lead in this context to an evaluative research paradigm. The classical planning of experiments with intervention and control groups is possible only in the most rare cases. Effect analyses of training are the current adequate investigation instrumentarium. The change in effects of a training and competitive system is primarily oriented to international top performances. Consequently, state-of-the-art analyses are a systematic characteristic mode of working. The following research strategies may be differentiated according to content:

- process accompanying training and competition research

- preparatory research (goal or foundationally oriented) with claims to knowledge, generalization or innovation
- development of measurement and information systems for research methods
- technology development.

The various aspects of research strategies prove that research in elite sport shows a complex character and not much teamwork between scientists and coaches on the one hand as well as athletes on the other. Research in elite sport requires interdisciplinary investigations. Interdisciplinarity is characterized by the following points:

- systematic cooperation of different disciplines
- target adequacy of common theories and methods.

Cooperation with coaches and athletes forges links between theory and practice. Process accompanyment should be directed toward:

- systematic cooperation of theory and practice
- common strategy in training and competition analyses.

3 Organizational and structural specifics in Germany

The research landscape for elite sport in Germany is based on institutes of both the old Federal Republic and former GDR. The following characteristics are to be distinguished:

In the old Federal Republic there existed more than 60 sport science institutes at universities. The research groups were comparatively small (with the exception of the German Sport University in Cologne). The types of investigations were predominantly preparatory research.

In the former German Democratic Republic there were two great research institutes for elite sport in Berlin (FES) and in Leipzig (FKS), respectively. The types of investigations were applied research.

The institute in Berlin (FES) is now responsible for training and competitive equipment. The institute in Leipzig (IAT) is a new establishment as of 1992. The staff of 80 persons is responsible for research in the field of training science. Both institutes are integrated into the research landscape for elite sport in Germany. The daily advising is incumbent on the Olympic centers (OSP) of the various federal states. Topics for all institutions are

addressed in the context of projects. They distinguish:
- university projects (preparatory and applied research)
- projects of non-university institutions (applied interdisciplinary sport specific research at the IAT and sport specific development of training and competitive equipment at the FES)
- projects of scientifically oriented advising at the Olympic centers (scientific advising for training and competition).

The coordination of research projects falls to a super-institutional coordinating group. The evaluation of research projects is organized by the BISp (the assigned officials of the responsible state ministry). Applications for new and continuing projects are annually reviewed by experts. Information concerning all projects is annually published by the BISp using standardized formats. Scientific and training experts evaluate project results.

The professional oversight of the OSP is conducted by the German Sports Federation (DSB). The efficiency evaluation of science-oriented advising is conducted by sports associations and committees of the German Sports Federation (DSB). The organizational structure can be characterized as a scientific alliance system. It is primarily directed towards optimization and the support of sport-specific training and competitive systems.

4 Object-oriented preparatory research

The purpose of this type of research is primarily directed toward knowledge. These investigations are frequently designed as to sequence prior to scientific advising, but there is a transfer between both scientific working methods. Two examples show the importance of object-oriented preparatory research in elite sport.

4.1 General and specific problems of force and power
There are many investigations and results to the topics force and power in elite sport. Substantial results have come in the past to following fields:

- Force dimension analysis (BÜHRLE, 1985)
- Muscular performance threshold and mechanical power (LEHNERTZ and PAMPUS, 1988)
- Stretch-shortening cycle (KOMI, 1984; GOLLHOFER, 1987).

It seems to be the case that the development of modern training methods is increasingly a matter of improving event-specific training and performance structures. General results have lost their influence on event-specific training methods. Hence various conditions have an effect on take-off in different kinds of sport, e.g., Fig. skating, gymnastics and diving (Table 1).

Table 1. Some parameters for take-off in Fig. skating, gymnastics and diving.

	Figure skating	Gymnastics		Diving			
		Acrobatic	Vault	Springboard		Platform	
				Stand	Approach	Stand	Approach
Approach velocity [m/s]	8-10	4,8-5,5	7,5-8,4	0	0,05-2	0	2-3
Time take-off [s]	0,12-0,16	0,11-0,13	0,09-0,11	0,3-0,5	0,25-0,45	0,17-0,25	0,09-0,15
min knee angle [°]	90-110	140-150	140-150	100	120	80	100
min hip angle [°]	90-110	120-130	85-95	90	105	90	120
Working angle knee [°]	40-60	30-40	30-40	60-70	45-55	50-70	40-60
Working angle hip [°]	50-60	50-60	50-60	30-40	50-60	50-60	30-40
Flight height CM [m]	0,60-0,65	1,70	1,00	1,20	2,00	0,55	0,50
rel. angular momentum [Nms]	20-26	115	90	65	70	65	70
Characteristic of the surface	stiff	elastic surface	elastic springboard	elastic springboard		stiff	

The question for the case of a take-off on an elastic springboard was, were there the same characteristics in the stretch-shortening cycle ? A few investigations in gymnastics showed differences. Using a special measurement system for acrobatic jumps in gymnastics (3 dynamometric platforms, EMG of 8 relevant muscle and vidiometric methods), WITT and KNOLL (1995) interpreted their results as a tension-shortening cycle.

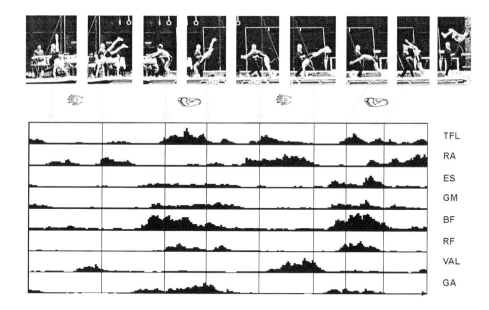

Fig. 1.   Relationship between sequences of the acrobatic jump and muscular activity
          (WITT and KNOLL, 1995).

Investigations of the take-off in horse vaulting in gymnastics showed
similar results. At the World Championships in Gymnastics in 1997 about
300 athletes were analyzed with a measurement system for horse vaulting
(Fig. 2).

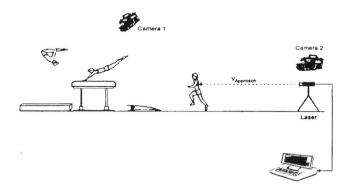

Fig. 2.   Measuring system for horse vault.

Top athletes were additionally recorded by a high speed video system
(250 Hz). The progression of the knee and the hip angle were analyzed

(Fig. 3).

Fig. 3 shows that top athletes carry out their take-off on the elastic springboard in a very short time interval. In the 0.1 second interval the angle difference of the knee and hip joint amounts to 20 degrees. The progression of hip and knee angle certified that the motion on the springboard is more a tension-shortening cycle than a stretch-shortening cycle.

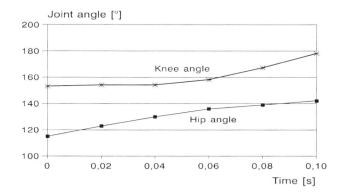

Fig. 3.   The progression of knee and hip angle on the elastic springboard

In some cases event-specific measurement and information systems developed into a landmark of training methodology. These were an effective way to check the performance in combat sports (TUENNEMANN, 1996). The following objectives of movement simulations and application of adequate simulators have been pursued:

For obtaining objective values on selected parameters of wrestling specific strength under almost competition-like conditions,

for obtaining information on the actual level of performance during the process of loading (on-line) and to guarantee athlete biofeedback,

to produce a load impetus to simulate competition conditions (TUENNE-MANN, 1996).

The throw simulator in wrestling (Fig. 4) is an example of an event-specific measuring system.

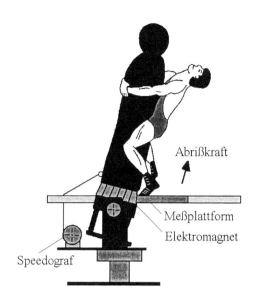

Fig. 4.   Throw simulator in wrestling (TUENNEMANN, 1996).

Another example in wrestling is the roll-over simulator (TUENNEMANN, 1996). The maximum strength applied can be measured for this standard technique in wrestling (Fig. 5).

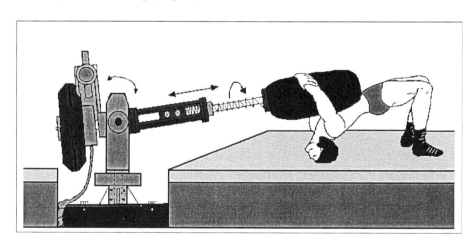

Fig. 5.   Roll-over simulator

4.2 Coordination in rapid rotational movements

Airborne human rotational movements represent a complicated problem of theoretical mechanics. Many studies have been presented during recent years by YEADON (1984, 1993) and HILDEBRAND (1985) and other authors to gain new knowledge of mechanic principles. In state-of-the-art analyses of the last Olympic cycles we investigated the take-off and angular velocity in different disciplines (Table 2). Rapid airborne rotations call for a high level of training methods. Investigations (KRUG and WITT, 1996) proved that this is also a problem of motor control. Using EEG procedures we could verify that active movement imagery is an important part of learning complicated airborne rotations. Electromyographical studies showed different muscular activities during twisting somersaults in diving and gymnastics and jumps with rapid rotations in Fig. skating.

	Transversal axis	Longitudinal axis	Twisting somersaults (Longitudinal axis)
Diving	1300 (3 1/2 salto fwd)		1385 (1½ bwd with 4½ twist)
Gymnastics	1200 (double salto fwd horse vault)		
Figure skating		1800 (quadruple Toeloop)	
Sport acrobatics			1500 (4 time twist)
Trampolining			1600 (7 time twist)

In Fig. skating KNOLL and HILDEBRAND (1996) demonstrated the influence of the angle between longitudinal axis and direction of angular momentum on an efficient use of the produced angular momentum. Analyses of different triple Axels (Fig. 6) prove that jumps have a good stability if the longitudinal axis has only an insignificant tilt in the landing position.

Fig. 6.   Kinegram of a triple Axel in Fig. skating (KNOLL and HILDE-BRAND, 1996).

But not only the relationship between angular momentum and longitudinal axis determines a good flight and landing. The investigations prove that the general direction of angular momentum is very important.

5 Process-accompanying training and competition research

The key issue for further enhancement of performance is improvement of training efficiency. There are many aspects for increasing efficiency. Hence the international transfer of know-how by coaches and athletes continuously increases. Yet there are not many international scientific projects. Therefore, international scientific cooperation in the field of process-accompanying training and competition research should be promoted. Two examples in this direction are described.

5.1 The FILA project in wrestling
The modern communication systems (multimedia, internet) point the way to the future. The outlook concerning use of a multimedia database in several kinds of sports is positive. The International Wrestling Federation (FILA) supports the project of a multimedia database. Considering state-of-the-art analyses of recent years, the IAT developed a CD with following database:

• results of all international wrestling events
• statistics on more than 14000 wrestlers
• 375 video clips and 1000 photos of famous wrestlers
• multimedia presentations of wrestling techniques.

This database exists also on the IAT homepage (URL: FILA-Wrestling.org). Since July 19, 1997 about 78000 scannings have been registered. Besides the international project in wrestling, on the IAT homepage are also multimedia databases for weightlifting and triathlon. Following facts in weightlifting (URL: WeightliftingData.org) are integrated:

- results of the most weightlifting events
- statistics on more than 5577 weight lifters
- 786 video clips and 85 photos
- multimedia presentations of weightlifting techniques.

Since September 20, 1997 about 34000 scannings have been registered. The multimedia database in triathlon is being set up.

5.2 The ISBS projects in gymnastics

These projects made it possible for international scientific groups to use dynamometric and video recordings from the 1994 and 1997 World Championships in Gymnastics at the Institute for Applied Training Science (IAT). The investigations were also certified as ISBS projects.

In comparison with analyses of former World Championships and European Championships of juniors the purposes of the investigation were directed at:

- first to provide recommendations for learning/perfecting elements
- secondly to reflect on dangers and risks.

Specific kinemetric measuring methods depending on the problem (2D or 3D procedures) were used. In state-of-the-art analyses, the height of flight elements was evaluated. In a first step an estimated value of the height of flight (time of flight) was calculated. In the second step CG heights were measured by photogrammetric procedures. Dynamometrical measurements of apparatus reaction forces combined with special measuring systems were applied on the horizontal bar and uneven bars (KNOLL, DRENK and KRUG, 1996) to differentiate between gymnastics performances by juniors and seniors and between women and men. Mathematical models (KNAUF, 1986) were used to calculate resultant joint moments of acrobatic jumps.

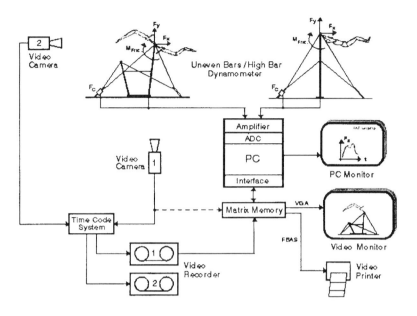

Fig. 7.   Measuring system for horizontal bar and uneven bars.

The investigation showed the necessity of developing special training programs for juniors aimed at improvement in endurance, strength, speed and coordination. In these programs, basic structures - e.g., giant swings, flic-flac, take-off movements and saltos with and without turns - should play an important role. Simultaneously, it is necessary to train the following basic abilities:

- power for take-off movements as well as for flexion and extension movements
- adaptation to fast turns around longitudinal and transversal axis preparations for landing.

All recommendations for a higher level abilities should be combined with the demands in order to reflect biological peculiarities and reduce risks for juvenile athletes. Interestingly, the results of the 1994 and 1997 ISBS projects proved to be very helpful to the Technical Committees and Working Groups of the International Gymnastics Federation (FIG).

6 Future demands on research and training

In the final evaluation of the object-oriented preparatory research as well as process-accompanying training and competition research in elite sport we create the sequence model of effects within the training and competition system. This model is shown in Fig. 8.

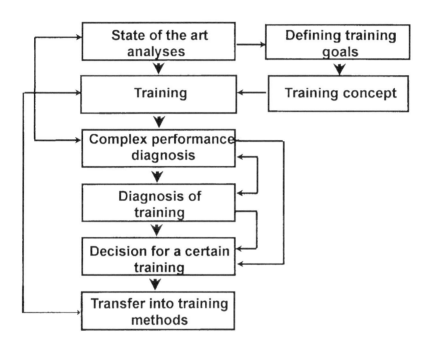

Fig. 8.   Sequence model of effects within the training and competition system.

In summary, substantial future demands on research and training are focused on:

• enhancing performance demands
• extensive scientific control and coaching risk reduction should be one of the major issues of scientific projects
• scientific control should be also extended to young athletes training
• exchange processes in the scientific field of elite sport are to be extended.

7 References

BOUCHOUT, J.-P. (1993). Political and social conditions of elite sport in Europe. In MESTER, J. (Ed.). 2nd European forum "Sport science in Europe 1993". Cologne, September 8-12, 1993.

BÜHRLE, M. (1985). Dimensionen des Kraftverhaltens und ihre spezifischen Trainingsmethoden. In BÜHRLE, M. (Hrsg.). Grundlagen des Maximal- und Schnellkrafttrainings. Schorndorf.

GOLLHOFER, A. (1987). Schnellkraftleistungen im Dehnungs-Verkürzungs-Zyklus. Erlensee.

HILDEBRAND, F. (1985). Eine biomechanische Analyse der Drehbewegungen des menschlichen Körpers. Leipzig, Habilitation.

KNAUF, M. (1986). Biomechanische Modellierung und Bewegungs-simulation mit Hilfe von Gliederketten unter Berücksichtigung elastischer Widerlager - ein Beitrag zur Weiterentwicklung der Modellmethode in der Biomechanik. Leipzig, Habilitation.

KNOLL, K. and HILDEBRAND, F. (1996). Angular momentum in jumps with rotations on the longitudinal axis in Fig. skating- 3D- analysis and computer simulation. In ABRANTES, J. (Ed.). Proceedings XIV Symposium on Biomechanics in Sports. June 25-29, 1996, Madeira, Portugal.

KNOLL, K. DRENK, V. and KRUG, J. (1996). Dynamometric measuring procedures for horizontal bar and uneven bars. In ABRANTES, J. (Ed.). Proceedings XIV Symposium on Biomechanics in Sports. June 25-29, 1996, Madeira, Portugal.

KOMI, P. V. (1984). Physiological and biomechanical correlates of muscle function: effects of muscle structure and stretch-shortening cycle on force and speed. In TERJUNG, R. L. (Ed.). Exercise and Sport Science Reviews. Vol. 12, pp. 81-121. Lexington, Mass.

KRUG, J. and WITT, M. (1996). Motor learning and muscular request for rapid air-borne rotations of athletes. In ABRANTES, J. (Ed.). Proceedings XIV Symposium on Biomechanics in Sports. June 25-29, 1996, Madeira, Portugal.

KUHN, T. S. (1962). The structure of scientific revolutions. Chicago.

MARTIN, D.; KRUG, J.; REIß, M. and ROST, K. (1996). Entwicklungs-tendenzen im Spitzen- und Nachwuchssport : Weltstandsanalysen-Probleme-Folgerungen mit einem Plädoyer für die Chancengleichheit deutscher Sportlerinnen und Sportler. In Zeitschrift für Angewandte Trainingswissenschaft 2/96.

LEHNERTZ, K. and PAMPUS, B. (1988). Trainingssteuerung im Rudern anhand muskelphysiologischer Parameter. In STEINACKER,†J. M. (Hg.), Rudern - sportmedizinische und sportwissenschaftliche Aspekte. Berlin - Heidelberg.

TUENNEMANN, H. (1996). Means, methods and results of training control in combat sports. In DAVIDOV, H. (Ed.). The process of training and competition in view of the 96 Atlanta games. The Second post Olympic international symposium, Netanya, Israel, December 28-30, 1996.

WILLIMCZIK, K. (1985). Interdisziplinäre Sportwissenschaft-Forderungen an ein erstarrtes Konzept. In Sportwissenschaft 15 (1985) 1, 9-32.

WITT, M. and KNOLL, K. (1995). Untersuchungen zur Optimierung der Absprungbewegungen in der Sprungreihe'Rondat-Flick-Flack-Doppelsalto'. In KRUG, J. and MINOW, H.-J. (Hrsg.). Sportliche Leistung und Training. Sankt Augustin.

YEADON, M. R. (1984). The mechanics of twisting somersaults. Loughborough, Doctoral Thesis.

YEADON, M. R. (1993). The biomechanics of twisting somersaults. Part I: Rigid body motions. In Journal of Sport Science, 11, 187-198.

5

SCIENCE AND SERVICE IN ELITE SPORTS IN FINLAND - ORGANIZATIONAL, INFRASTRUCTURAL AND FINANCIAL ASPECTS

J.T. VIITASALO
Vice director
Research Institute for Olympic Sports
Jyväskylä, Finland

Keywords: Finland, health sciences, KIHU, service, social sciences.

History and background

Elite sport is a solid part of Finnish sports culture. Finnish athletes have been very successful in international competitions since the independence in the year of 1917. Finland is still the most successful country in the century-long history of Olympic sports, when the number of medals won by each country is proportioned to the country's population. Finns have won a total of 135 gold, 123 silver and 155 bronze Olympic medals. To day there are around 3000 Finnish top athletes who compete at national level and 300 to 400 national team athletes who have represented Finland internationally for many years. There are 30 to 40 Finnish international sports stars.

Science in sports has been conducted in several institutions and centers in Finland for more than 50 years. At the beginning this work was based more or less on activities and interests of individual researchers, not that much on the interests and goals of the institutions themselves. One of the Finnish pioneers was Professor Martti J. Karvonen, who started to study endurance athletes in the Finnish Institute of Occupational Health in Helsinki nearly fifty years ago. Since then projects connected also with top sport has been conducted in the mentioned Finnish Institute as well as in the six Regional Institutes of Occupational Health.

In Finland we have universities in ten cities - Helsinki, Turku, Lappeenranta, Tampere, Jyväskylä, Vaasa, Kuopio, Joensuu, Oulu and Rovaniemi. In their faculties and departments occasionally many research projects connected also with elite sports have been executed. In five universities (Helsinki, Turku, Tampere, Kuopio and Oulu) there is a faculty of medicine. In those faculties as well as in the Universal and Central

Hospitals research work has been done for example in the field of sport medicine, especially in traumatology.

In 1985 sports and exercise medicine was approved as a medical specialty in Finland. After a six-year program in medicine, the student may enter one of eight residency positions available in the sports-medicine program. Training of the new doctors is executed in the Research Center for Sport and Health Science (LIKES) in Jyväskylä and in five sports-medicine research institutions founded by the Ministry of Education. These Institutions locate in Helsinki (Research Institute for Sports and Exercise Medicine), Turku (Sports Research Unit of the Paavo Nurmi Centre), Tampere (Research Institute for Sports and Exercise Medicine), Kuopio (Research Institute of Exercise Medicine) and Oulu (Department of Sports Medicine of Deaconess Institute of Oulu). In addition to research, all six institutions engage in training and informational activity and offer physicians' and testing services. The number of people working in each of these centers is between 10 - 20.

University of Jyväskylä

The position of sport science research in Finland was stabilized in the early 1960s, when instruction and research activities in sport science were shifted from Helsinki to the University of Jyväskylä, whose Faculty of Sport and Health Sciences became independent in 1968. Jyväskylä University has also the Faculty of Humanistics, Education, Social Sciences and Mathematics, and Natural Sciences.

The key areas of training and research carried out in the Faculty of Sport and Health Sciences are physical activity and health. The multidiciplinary foundations of the Faculty create a good basis for fruitful interactions in carrying out the basic functions to train specialists and to undertake research and development. The Faculty trains specialists in different areas of physical culture such as school sports, coaching, and sport planning and administration. Specialists in health education, physiotherapy, physical rehabilitation and public health education also graduate from the Faculty. Altogether the Faculty has 1100 full-day students and 160 employers in it's four departments - Physical Education, Biology of Physical Activity, Social Sciences of Sports, and Health Sciences.

The Department of Physical Education

The Department of Physical Education has the main responsibility for the training of teachers of physical education. Graduates qualify as teachers of physical and health education. The Department's primary teaching function in sport sciences is in the field of sport pedagogy and sport psychology. The former deals with the didactics of physical education and other pedagogical theory as well as the teaching of the relevant physical skills and teaching methodology. A new area of specialization recently introduced is that of dance pedagogy and in adapted physical education.

The Department of Biology of Physical Activity
The Department of Biology of Physical Activity offers courses in two specialized areas: Biomechanics and Exercise Physiology. These areas are well represented in the various curricula, such as coaching, physiotherapy and fitness testing. In addition, the Department is responsible for teaching the basic biomedical sciences to all students in the faculty.

Already in the early 1970s the Department decided to develop research in two main areas: Exercise Physiology and Biomechanics. Both have one full and one associate professorship. Research in the Department concentrates on the basic interaction between Physical Performance and Biological Factors of the Human Body. This major problem is investigated through two research programs: Biomechanics and Exercise Physiology. Both of these fields have various subareas, although the Department's principle is to avoid strict definitions and the division of either major field. Thus, it is frequently the practice to utilize methods from both biomechanics and physiology simultaneously for a specific research problem.

Another major principle in the Department's research work is to give equal emphasis to basic and applied research problems in Exercise Biology. In order to carry out successful research work in applied problems (e.g. sport, physiotherapy, ergonomics, etc.) the Department devotes about 50% of its research projects to problems, which could be classified as Basic Research in Exercise Biology. On the other hand, research in Exercise Biology must show good interaction with methodological developments in the basic sciences. Given its research policy the Department thus feels able to contribute strongly to the various applied fields related to Exercise Biology.

In basic research in Exercise Biology the Department concentrates on Mechanisms and Adaptation of Neuromuscular Function in Exercise. This area utilizes methods and ideas from both biomechanics (e.g. muscle mechanics, neuromuscular control) and exercise physiology (e.g. bio-chemistry, histochemistry).

The Department of Biology of Physical Activity is located in two separate buildings. The teaching laboratories are situated in the faculty building. The main research facilities moved into a modern research building in 1990 together with the research teams of the Department of Health Sciences. In this new complex the research facilities include 1750m^2 of laboratory space. The separate laboratories contain facilities for biochemistry, biomechanics and exercise physiology research. Each laboratory is equipped with the most modern research apparatus. The laboratory building has also modern facilities for electrical and mechanical workshops as well as for data processing.

The Department of Social Sciences of Sport
The Department of Social Sciences of Sport has the main responsibility for the training of specialists in the area of administration, planning and research in the field of sports and leisure. Graduates mainly find employment in public positions in sport and leisure administration and in sports organizations. The Department's primary teaching tasks in sport sciences are in sport sociology, sport administration and planning, and the social sciences of sport and leisure in general.

The Department of Health Sciences
The Department of Health Sciences has the main responsibility for the training of students in health sciences and teacher training in health sciences. Physiotherapy students are trained in cooperation with the Department of Biology of Physical Activity. Graduates in physiotherapy can expect to find leading positions in physiotherapy, public health and rehabilitation or other posts in training, directing and research in the field of physiotherapy; graduate teachers in physiotherapy are qualified as teachers in institutions in this field. Graduates in gerontology may find work in research or in training, directing and research positions in the care of elderly people and social and health care systems. Opportunities for graduates in health education at MSc level exist in both training, directing, and planning health care and health education and in research. The Department's primary teaching function in sport sciences is in the field of health sciences (public health, sports medicine, health education). The Department of Health Sciences is, in cooperation with the Faculty of Medicine in the University of Kuopio, one of the training centers for specialists in sports medicine.

Other facilities

In the Finnish sport organization 11 national and 3 regional Sport Institutes and Finnish Defense Forces' Sport School in Lahti have their own important role. Most of these institutes have good possibilities to make various tests of the physical performance characteristics e.g. many institutions have exercise lab in order to measure maximal oxygen consumption using a direct method and to determine blood variables. They also have good facilities to offer for training of the Finnish athletes. The sport institutes offer basic and supplementary professional education, club training for sports organizations, camps for competitive athletes, recreational programs for schools and work communities, and courses for fitness enthusiasts, special-need groups and recreational athletes. Some 160 promising men and women have the opportunity each year to complete their military service (all Finnish men are obliged to serve slightly less than a year) at the Sport School of the Finnish Defense Forces in Lahti. The athletes are thus assured of training facilities adequate to help them get to the top in their sports.

The dissemination of information is an essential extension of research activity. In Finland, national and international sport-science information services were launched and systematized in the early 1960's. The information service of the University of Jyväskylä Library, the Finnish Society for Research in Sport and Physical Education (Helsinki), the Sports Library of Finland's information service (Helsinki), the UKK Institute's information service (Tampere), the LIKES information service (Jyväskylä), and the sports libraries associated with Finland's sport institutes all specialize in the dissemination of sport-science information.

New plans

As described above Finland has several organizations and institutions which work in the field of public health, physical activity and sometimes also of top sport. In Finland the national Olympic committee together with the national sports federations is responsible for the international success of the Finnish athletes. In the middle of 1980's the Finnish Olympic committee was not, however, satisfied with the success in top sport and prepared a plan to improve coaching of the Finnish elite athletes. Among other things there were four important items in the plan:

• we should have more sports schools in Finland

- the Finnish elite athletes should receive state salary
- new training centers should be build in Finland
- a new research institute should be established.

At the moment all those hopes have been fulfilled more or less. For athletically inclined young people, Finland has developed an educational system that offers a change to combine a full program of studies with sports training. Finland opened it's first sports-oriented upper secondary schools in 1986. Nowadays the number of such schools is 12, all with general nationwide enrollment. Five of the schools specialize in a specific sport. Each school attends to both normal academic instruction and training facilities. At present the schools have a total enrollment of about 1400 young athletes representing 35 different sports. At 14 vocational institutes, Finland has combined vocational training and sport careers, in the form of so-called sport classes. Training facilities in the vicinity of these schools are excellent, so that the athletes are helped in the accomplishment of their goals. The study program meanwhile assures the pupil of a vocation when his or her athletic career is over. The time spent in training is not accepted towards the vocational diploma.

At the moment 13 athletes in winter events and 17 in summer events receive a grant (or salary) of 5000 FIM per months from the Finnish Ministry of Education. All these athletes are near the international top in their sports events and they are considered as potential medal winners in the next Olympics.

The Finnish elite sport coaching system is nowadays supported by a network of four national training centers. The sport institutes of Vierumäki, Kuortane, Vuokatti and Pajulahti were nominated National Training Centers in 1989. They offer coaching and education programs for athletes and coaches in their respective sports.

The National Training Center of Kuortane has specialized in athletics, wrestling, shooting, and artistic gymnastics but also serves athletes in swimming, archery, skiing, biathlon, basketball, volleyball, orienteering and weightlifting. The special field of interest of Kuortane is the study of the speed-strength aspects of athletic performance and athletes' recovery. There is a recovery station at the Institute comprising a physiotherapy center with water therapy facilities, saunas, and relaxation rooms.

The National Training Center of the Finnish Sport Institute Vierumäki serves athletes and coaches in ice hockey, basketball, athletics, tennis, golf, and squash with special emphasis being placed on custom-made training session packages, coaches' national examination syllabus, and athletes' career planning. In co-operation with the sports medicine station LUNSA, Vierumäki serves athletes of both elite and recreational sports.

The National Training Center of Vuokatti is the headquarters of the Finnish elite coaching in skiing, ski jumping, Nordic combined, and biathlon. The Vuokatti Ski Training Center, and the Vuokatti Sports Hotel serve Finland' National and Junior Ski Teams providing them with outstanding training, educational and housing facilities.

The National Training Center of Pajulahti has specialized in the study of training facility development, and in coaches' and sport instructors' education. Badminton, karate, wrestling, and athletics are the particular fields of interest at Pajulahti.

Research Institute for Olympic Sports (KIHU)

One item in the plan of the Finnish Olympic Committee was to establish a new research institute for elite sports in Finland. KIHU was established in the spring of 1990 by the Finnish Foundation for the Promotion of Physical Education and Health, and is supported by the Finnish Ministry of Education and the Finnish Olympic Committee. KIHU activities are managed by its own Executive Board whose members represent the above organizations, Sports Federations and the University of Jyväskylä.

The overall goals of KIHU include interdisciplinary research and applied service. Interdisciplinary research into top performance in sports is aimed at 1) examining biomechanical, physiological, medical, psychological and sociological aspects of training, competition and coaching in individual and team sports and 2) at development of testing and coaching methods, educational materials, training aids and equipment.

Applied services promote successful performance of top athletes, coaches, teams and sports federation by 1) consulting and practical assistance to sports organizations, educational and training centers in charge of coaching education, as well as to the sporting goods industry 2) information search, up-date and state-of-the art reviews of problem areas and 3) special courses and intensive training seminars for coaches, athletes, sports scientists and administrators.

The annual operating budget of KIHU is 4.3 million FIM and is provided from the Ministry of Education. The full time staff hired by this budget consists of four senior researchers, two junior researchers, five research assistants, five technicians and a secretary. Research positions run for 2-5 year terms. Additional funding for research projects and service (totally about 3 million FIM) comes from Sports Federations, the Finnish Olympic Committee, Jyväskylä Science Park, the Technology Development Center of Finland and private companies. This allows KIHU to hire 12-15 additional assistants.

KIHU facilities include the Hippos sports and research complex of the city of Jyväskylä on the University campus with office space (800m² for KIHU), an indoor 200 m track facility, several ball game and gymnastics halls, 2 ice hockey rinks (all equipped for research, training and competition). Research laboratories, a library and computer center of the University of Jyväskylä are provided for KIHU by special agreement. Additional "on-site" research facilities in the city of Jyväskylä are Harju Sports Stadium, the indoor ice hockey arena, the speed skating track, the skiing center at Laajavuori, an Olympic size swimming pool, out-door artificial ice stadium and Graniitti Shooting Center.

KIHU operates closely with the Finnish Olympic Committee, the Sports Federations, Sports Institutes and Training Centers, the University of Jyväskylä and the Faculty of Sport and Health Sciences, the Sports Medicine and Sports Psychology Units as well as with the other Educational and Research Institutions, Sport Clubs and private companies in Finland. During the past few years, co-operation and joint projects with foreign Research Institutes and Universities have increased. KIHU is actively involved in the worldwide network of sports science research e.g. by publishing in international journals and participating and lecturing in international congresses.

References

Sport and Physical Education in Finland. Eds. Palkama, M. and Nieminen, L. The Finnish Society for Research in Sport and Physical Education, Forssan Kirjapaino Oy., Forssa, 1997.

Brochures by :

The Finnish Olympic Committee
The Faculty of Sport and Health Sciences, University of Jyväskylä
The Department of Biology of Physical Activity, University of Jyväskylä
The Research Institute for Olympic Sports, Jyväskylä

6

ARE AUSTRIAN ELITE ATHLETES GIVEN SCIENTIFIC SUPPORT?

E. KORNEXL
Institute of Sports Sciences, University of Innsbruck, Austria

Keywords: ABS, Austria, IMSB, ÖISM, scientific support, sports medicine, sports science.

1 Problem Area

International developments in elite sports have also found their way across Austria´s borders. Looking for ways and means to increase performance results in the call for including scientific knowledge and research. What is the situation concerning scientific support for elite athletes in Austria? This question will be dealt with in three parts in the following. At the beginning there will be a summary about Austrian institutions scientifically supporting Austrian elite athletes with a description of their tasks and possibilities. Afterwards there will be a critical overview presenting strong and weak points of these institutions regarding the task of scientific support in order to draw concrete conclusions for improvement in the situation in Austria in the final part.

country	total	summer
Austria:	1.97 / 1 mill. inhabitants	0.26 / 1 mill. inhabitants
Germany:	1.23 / 1 mill. inhabitants	0.89 / 1 mill. inhabitants
Switzerland:	1.91 / 1 mill. inhabitants	0.59 / 1 mill. inhabitants
U.S.A.:	0.42 / 1 mill. inhabitants	0.40 / 1 mill. inhabitants
Norway:	5.30 / 1 mill. inhabitants	1.44 / 1 mill. inhabitants

Fig. 1.   Number of medals related to inhabitants (average of 3 Olympic years). Olympic medals per 1 million inhabitants (1988 - 1996).

The introduction to this topic, Fig. 1 shows an overview of Austrian athletes´ achievements compared to those of other countries. It presents an exemplary analysis of medals won at the Olympic Games per 1 million inhabitants. Winter and Summer Games can be looked at separately or together. The figures present the average number of medals per 1 million inhabitants per Olympic year and per country.

Austria has achieved a successful result and lies - compared to other countries - somewhere in the upper midfield. One has to admit, however, that this above-average picture is caused by especially achievements in alpine sports. From this one could infer that the situation concerning scientific support seems to be „not so bad at all".

For a precise answer to the questions asked at the beginning one has to define the concept of „scientific support". The first answer may point to scientific support concerning the process to optimum performance. In this case it is useful to look at the factors determining performance in sports which are to be optimized (s. Fig. 2).

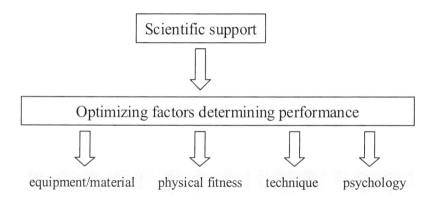

Fig. 2   Model for scientific support.

According to this the concept of „scientific support" means both
• providing the latest insights into knowledge about optimizing performance and
• support by specific research projects concerning questions within the process of optimizing performance.

2 Institutions for Scientific Support

In Austria support of elite sports is established in the „Law for Sports Promotion" (1969): „Places for sports medical and sports specific research, consultation, examination, and treatment with an all-Austrian significance are worth promoting".

The amount of public funds for scientific support within Austrian elite sports cannot be determined at the moment because

a) sports funds allotment does not consider this recipient separately
b) a distinction between scientific and non-scientific support is very difficult: a few examples from the governmental budget with at least a certain reference to scientific support:
ca. 15 mill. ATS / year for trainers´ payment and advanced education
ca. 8 mill. ATS / year subsidy of the IMSB and scientific coordinators at the departments of sports science at the universities
ca. 8 mill. ATS / year support funds for the Elite Sports Committee (only partial promotion of scientific support)

In Austria there are several institutions realizing this scientific support for top athletes, either directly or indirectly, to varying degrees and with varying emphasis. The following survey also contains trainers, who pass on their knowledge of scientific coaching (gained during their own education) to the athletes and thus give them - at least to a certain extent - scientific support.

2.1 Trainers

The extent of scientific knowledge and the critical faculty of the trainers in coaching athletes is crucially determined by their level of education and advanced training. Recent investigations about Austrian trainers confirm the call for further expansion of education based on science and sport-specific specialization. For example, 75% of the interviewees would appreciate university education (BSO, Federal Chancellor´s Bureau, Trainer Situation in Austria, Enquete, Vienna 1997, p. 20). Another point of consideration is the extension of trainer education. In Germany, for example, the number of educational lessons is twice as high as in Austria.

2.2 Institute for Medical and Sport-Scientific Consultation (IMSB)

The IMSB is an association whose aim is to be a place of scientific service for Austrian sports associations and elite athletes. It is supported by the Austrian state with an annual subsidy of approximately 7 mill. ATS.

At present the IMSB has 10 full-time employees with sport-specific or sports-medical education. Another 10 experts with scientific education have consultancy contracts.

Offering scientific support to elite athletes includes:

- sports medical care: the IMSB is connected to a net of 17 sports-medical check-up points in Austria, where mainly basic sports medical examinations are given. Further special sports-medical parameters for optimal performance are diagnosed at the IMSB Center in the „Wiener Südstadt", where appropriate training recommendations are passed on to the athletes. In addition, they offer physiotherapeutic care via subsidies by the Association for Elite Sports.
- sports scientific support: the IMSB offers athletes elementary diagnostics of motor performance as a basis for consultation about special training supervision (incl. nutrition, anti-doping, and anthropometric measurements).

   At present a relevant fraction of sports associations and a number of elite athletes - especially those from the east of Austria and summer sports - are supported by the IMSB. The capacity of this institution allows support for athletes at their training locations, at training camps, and at competitions. The IMSB also organizes annual advanced trainer education. In this repect, the IMSB at present provides the greatest influence on support of scientific coaching in Austria.

2.3 Austrian Institute for Sports Medicine (ÖISM)

In close collaboration and partial overlap of personnel with the section for sports physiology in the Department of Sports Science at Vienna University, the ÖISM provides four medical doctors. Other experts can be consulted when required.

The ÖISM - similar to the IMSB - aims at sports-medical care for athletes in popular and elite sports.

Offerings:

- basic sports-medical examinations
- special analysis in the field of cardiologic and spirometric ergometries
- blood analysis
- force and velocity diagnostics

The main share of the parameters can be analysed in laboratory and field tests.

Training consultation and deduction of special measures in training supervision are offered.

At present several elite athletes and national squads from different kinds of sports are provided sport-medical support.

2.4   Association for Supporting Elite Sports (ABS)

The ABS is an association founded and financially supported by the federal states of Tyrol, Salzburg, and Vorarlberg. It runs a central office in Innsbruck, which deals with the various projects.

The aim of the ABS is the (scientific) promotion and support of elite sports in close collaboration with the sports medical departments in the federal states and with the departments of sports science at the universities of Innsbruck and Salzburg.

At present the main focus of scientific support lies in the fields of sports medicine, scientific coaching, technique-specific and biomechanical consultation and support. Concerning the various kinds of sports the main emphasis is on winter and alpine sports. The support mainly applies to the western region of Austria. Due to limited resources the possibilities of the ABS are - despite remarkable achievements - restricted.

2.5   Association of Austrian Sports Doctors - Sports medical Departments in the Federal States

Austrian athletes have the possibility of consulting ca. 700 holders of the general sports medical diploma and ca. 150 specialists with certificates for sports medical care at their practices, hospitals, or sports medical departments in the federal states. Apart from a few exceptions the main emphasis is on basic sports medical check-ups.

Related to the high number of sports medical doctors, the practical effects at the moment are - apart from a few commendable exceptions - rather poor. The reason is the lack of time and financial resources for supporting top athletes due to the obligatory general care of patients.

In most of the Austrian federal states there is a department of sport (and cardiovascular) medicine in one of the larger hospitals. These are in general the places where sport associations in the federal states can take medical tests. Many top athletes get at least a basic sports medical check-up.

2.6   Departments of Sport Science at the Universities of Vienna, Salzburg, Innsbruck, and Graz

In the course of implementing basic research within sport science (science of coaching, kinesiology, sport psychology and sociology, biomechanics, sports medicine, sport pedagogy), several projects of applied research and support within elite sports are carried out at these departments. There is a certain tendency towards winter sports and ball games. At present the main emphases concerning the direction of training-specific research and support are scarcely coordinated among the departments. They depend on the institute personnel´s fields of interest.

On the initiative of the Federal Chancellor´s Bureau each department has installed a full-time coordinator, who functions as a bridge between research and applied coaching. His task is to put the latest scientific knowledge into practice and - vice versa - to analyse problems of practical coaching scientifically. Valuable initiatives for elite sports have originated from this.

The departments are limited in employing their staff for practical coaching because of scarce personnel resources and the pressures of scientific research.

Indirectly the departments gain great influence on the scientific support of elite sports because an increasing number of trainers possess a sport scientific degree as a basis for further sport-specific specialization. In many kinds of sports the leading trainer positions are occupied by sport scientists.

2.7 Special Schools for Sport Performance Including Scientific Support:

Special schools for sport performance (e.g. Stams, Südstadt, Schladming, Eisenerz) gain increasing influence on elite sports, especially in sports education for young people. The carefully selected training personnel have good basic knowledge concerning scientific coaching. Without these centers one could not expect top performance in several kinds of sport.

3 A Critical View of Scientific Support - Strong and Weak Points

Despite the relatively high number of scientific departments, a critical observation produces the following results:

Scientific support re.	Strong / weak points
material / equipment	Research and support is almost exclusively in the hands of companies. There are problems regarding special requests, individual adaptions, and expensive new developments. Specific integration of universities and other research institutions would be useful.
physical fitness / motor performance ability, medical care	Despite some financial restrictions there are relatively broad possibilities for basic sports medical care. There are deficits, however, in basic sports medical research (genetics research, cell membrane research, muscle physiology ...).

Scientific support re.	Strong / weak points
physical fitness / motor performance ability, medical care	Despite remarkable initiatives (IMSB, ABS, ÖISM, some institutes in the federal states) in the area of sport-specific performance diagnostics and in the area of specific consultation concerning training supervision of motor performance parameters, this field requires a lot of improvement. Sport-specific performance tests with instant feedback need to be developed and improved.
technique (3D-analysis, instant feedback systems, force diagnostics ...)	Scientific support in the area of technique optimization shows a large deficit. Only a few supporting institutions are sufficiently equipped with equipment and staff for exact technique analysis. For future promotion this field has to be granted highest priority.

4 Consequences

The important measures for optimizing scientific support for Austrian elite athletes to be taken are therefore:

1. Intensification of advanced trainer education:
   The existing support institutions should be encouraged to offer more and improved advanced trainer education. These offers should consider relevant necessities and contain the possibility for those interested to join support projects. The Austrian Olympic Committee, the Federal Sports Organization, and the Federal Institutes for Physical Education should intensify comprehension and coordination of trainers´ needs.

2. **Expansion of institutions for consultation and research** with present emphasis on the fields of material/equipment, technique optimization, psychological performance parameters, and basic medical research. This is not going to be possible without considerable governmental personnel and financial support. The existing support institutions have to intensify the integration of relevant fields in science (technology, chemistry, psychology ...).

3. **Decentralization, cooperation, and useful concentration** of the existing support institutions:

In order to have well-equipped scientific support institutions within easy reach for all athletes there should be at least one each in western, southern and northeastern Austria. These institutions should both cooperate (perhaps emphasis according to kinds of sport or target areas) and compete in order to encourage optimization of outcome. Sports medical and training-specific support ought to collaborate more closely.

4. **Expansion of regional performance centers with scientific support:** The advantage of performance centers with a main focus on one kind of sport, especially if they are combined with school education, has definitely proven successful by sport performance results. Such centers should be increasingly established according to regional aspects and should be linked to sufficient scientific support. An evaluation by the Federal Sports Organization, the Austrian Olympic Committee, and the relevant sport-specific associations, including appropriate incentives for performance, would be necessary.

7
SPORTS-SCIENTIFIC SUPPORT AT THE FREIBURG OLYMPIC-TRAINING-CENTRE

A. SCHWIRTZ, A. NEUBERT, B. STAPELFELDT, M. HILLEBRECHT, A. GOLLHOFER, L. SCHWEIZER, U. WIEDMANN and M. BÜHRLE

Keywords: biomechanics, cc-skiing, Freiburg, Germany, olympic-training-centre, performance diagnostics, ski jumping.

1 Preliminary Remarks

The Freiburg-(Black-Forest) Olympic-Training-Centre (OTC) was established at the end of 1988 as one of 20 centres in Germany (see Fig. 1 and 2). At that time, six elite sport discipline associations belonged, comprising alpine skiing, nordic skiing, cycling sports, wrestling, track and field, gymnastics and disability sport. It had neither its own centre nor its own spaces for primary staff. Supporting integrated discipline associations is guaranteed through several cooperative agreements with facilities at the University of Freiburg, among others. The particular tasks for the accompanying sport-scientific measures derive from actual requirements of the represented associations. Although "only" six elite discipline associations are supported by the Freiburg-OTC, the number of individual disciplines within a particular type of sport, for example for track and field, an any case is much higher. A high degree of discipline-specific competence is an integral part of daily operation in biomechanical performance diagnostics, which can scarcely be matched by an individual person across all sport disciplines.

1 Berlin
2 Chemnitz/Dresden
3 Cottbus/Frankf./Oder
4 Frankf./Rhein-Main
5 Freiburg/Schwarzw.
6 Hamburg/Kiel
7 Hannover/Wolfsbg.

8 Köln/Bonn/Leverk.
9 Leipzig
10 Magdeburg/Halle
11 Mecklenbg./Vorp.
12 München
13 Potsdam
14 Rheinland-Pfalz/Saarl.

15 Rhein-Neckar
16 Rhein-Ruhr
17 Stuttgart
18 Tauberbischofsh.
19 Thüringen
20 Westfalen

Fig. 1.   Olympic-Training-Centres in Germany.

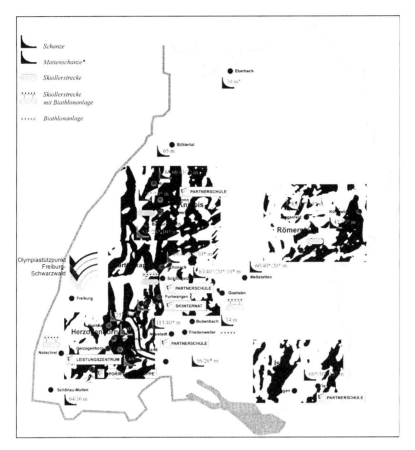

Fig. 2.   Regional establishment (Nordic skiing)of the OTC -Freiburg (Black-Forest).

2 The Freiburg concept of biomechanical advising

Years-long sport-scientific mentoring of various sport organizations by the
Institute for Sport and Sport Science at the University of Freiburg (Director:
Prof. Dr. M. Bührle) flowed into a cooperative agreement with the Freiburg-
Olympic-Training-Centre. From January 1989 on, it was possible to hire
an additional colleague in the area of biomechanics. Tasks assigned were
divided from a full position and distributed to an entire working group (7
colleagues, flexible personel availability, and ensured full utilization of
available equipment. Individual types of sport which are advised through
the OTC are assigned to specific colleagues. In general, these individuals
can be approached directly or contact can be established via the coordinator.
For complex investigations, several colleagues collaborate and can be further

supported by student assistants. The evaluation of data (for example in film analysis) is performed by the respectively qualified supporting staff. The balance vis-à-vis the OTC takes place on the basis of a cooperative contract for specific factors. An important component of this concept is additionally the possibility of utilizing electronical and mechanical labs in which specific equipment has been developed and usefully adapted for competitive sport contexts.

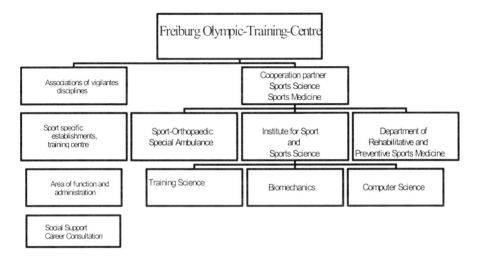

Fig. 3.   Structure of organizationof the OTC (cooperation institutes)

3   Tasks and possibilities in biomechanical performance diagnostic training direction

Scientific services are a central task in the concept of the Olympic Training Centre (see Fig. 3). Through these, the necessary conditions should be created for guaranteeing of optimal competitive sport conditions and to provide systematic scientific advising for athletes and trainers. The advising of athletes and trainers on the basis of objective results (performance diagnostics, empirical investigations, etc.) stands in the foreground.

In this context, advising is to be understood as "collaborative consi-deration" and the advisor seen as a "source of advise or as specialist colleague." Advising thus means to support someone through advice after collaborative consideration.

The following areas comprise the scope of biomechanics:

- Analysis of sport-motoric motion techniques, i.e. describing and esti-mation performance-relevant characteristics on the basis of kinemato-graphic (video, film), dynamographic (force measurement), electro-myographic (muscle activity, etc.) and anthropometric (body build characteristic) techniques.
- Performance of conditioning analysis, i.e. discipline-specific performance diagnostic investigations for estimating leg-, arm- and jump- force-capability on the basis of continually improved, years-tested diagnostic processes.
- Planning and collaboration of training and competitive support measure-ments (participation in courses of instruction, competitions, i.a.).
- Preventative biomechanics: Collaboration with sports medicine providers (see Fig. 3, orthopaedists, internists, performance physiologists) for prevention of injuries or for precise load directing.
- Documentation of training data: computer supported recording and analysis of training contents and methods.
- Development and maintenance of immediate information systems (qualitative video analysis, videoprinter).
- Advising of trainers and athletes in the writing of training schedules (technical and conditioning control, performance prognosis, load structuring).

4 Exemplary examples of support work

In the following three examples of concrete investigations for the OTC of the working group will be briefly shown. Data in the examples do not claim to be complete but are useful in illustrating the complex work.

4.1 Cycling: Intermuscular coordination and force development

For individual regulation and control of training it is necessary to have detailed knowledge of the athlete's specific strengths and weaknesses. In order to evaluate all basic conditional traits, an interdisciplinary approach using the methods of biomechanics and medicine is needed. Some studies in the field of cycling deal with the relation between electromyographical, dynamographical and physiological parameters in pedalling coordination. The aspect of alteration in EMG-parameters during an increase of load has rarely been the subject of scientific study (Jorge & Hull 1986, Kautz et. al., 1991, Taylor & Bronks 1995). The question is whether alterations can be found that point towards a change in coordination pattern at different work loads. As a consequence, a cyclist would have to use different cycling techniques in coping with different loads.

In the course of an interdisciplinary power diagnosis eight elite track cyclists underwent a ramp test (100/20/3) on a SRM-ergometer. At a cadence of 100 rpm they performed up to 440 Watt. Apart from the external load, lactate and oxygen absorption, the three pedal forces, the efficiency and the muscular activity of five leg muscles (tibialis anterior, gastrocnemius, vastus lateralis, rectus femoris and biceps femoris) were measured (see Fig. 4 and 5)

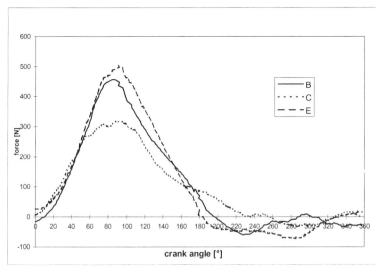

Fig. 4.   Typical effective force-angle-curves of three athletes (400 Watt, 100rpm).

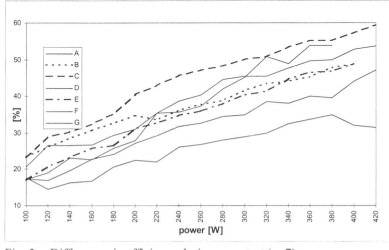

Fig. 5.   Differences in efficiency during ramp test (n=7).

In the context of this study not only mean values of the group, but also particular cases were of interest. The necessary parameters were deduced from the EMG graphs and the force graphs on every load level (mean average of 30 cycles). The cyclists worked at a load of 300 Watt with efficiency degrees between 35.8 and 60.8%. The maximal tangential forces exerted during that time lay between 340 and 420 N. The average maximum oxygen consumption was 65.4 ml/kg/min and the lactate value directly after the last load differed between 7.4 and 12.1 mmol/l. Even if the mean overall activity increased throughout all load levels, the time of activity of the single muscles differed greatly in some cyclists (examples in Fig. 6 and 7). Clearly there was no fixed EMG pattern for one particular load.

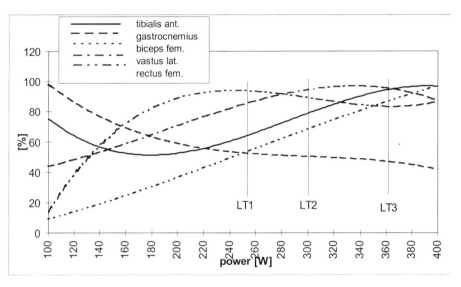

Fig. 6.   IEMG of 5 muscles (normalized to max. activity) and lactate thresholds (cyclist B).

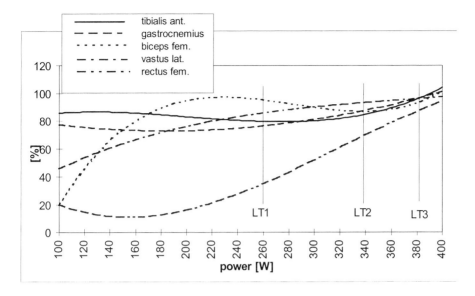

Fig. 7. IEMG of 5 muscles (normalized to max. activity) and lactate thresholds (cyclist E).

The strain and therefore the functional adaptation differs in every cyclist with the load. While the types of force and EMG patterns of every cyclist are typical for him, they can not be found to be all the same in all test subjects. This supports the necessity of an individual coaching.

4.2 Ski-jumping: Diagnosis of jumping performance and neuromuscular coordination

The sport scientific advice of top athletes in ski jumping takes into account not only senior top level athletes, but also juniors, to guarantee a systematical, long termed, continuos progression of young top athletes. We try to carry out this task by a differentiated performance diagnosis of the necessary abilities analysing the leg extension force. We want to verify the possibilities as well as the limits of this diagnosis in laboratory by comparing it with the results of a field study.

The basic performance diagnostics comprises a testing-battery for recording the ability of leg extension force (leg press, knee angle 70°, isometric and eccentric contraction) and the ability of jumping performance (standard jumping test, 3 forms of jumping: squat jump (SJ), counter movement jump (CMJ), drop jumps (DJ) from 24 and 32cm height). Apart from the abilities of maximal strength and of power, the ability of reactive strength is estimated by this test (BÜHRLE, 1989). The field study consisted in a complex biomechanical study performed during real ski jumps. 5 ski jumpers (national team) participated in this study conducted on the ski jump device in Oberwiesenthal. The following systems were used: a kinematic analysis (150 f/s, 2-d), electromyography (EMG) of 6 muscles and vertical force measurement with force plates inside the ski jump. From the basic strength and power measurements all registered parameters of the complex tests are transmitted to a database system. In table 1, the most important parameters of the 14 - 19 years old ski jumpers are collected.

Table 1. Mean-values from performance diagnosis for ski-jumpers with different ages.

age	14	15	16	17	18	19	Increase in %
n	19	29	32	34	13	10	14-19 years
height [cm]	165	170.6	174	178	178	180	9
weight [kg]	50.7	56.5	59.8	64.4	63.7	65.3	29
force max [N]	1219	1460	1530	1624	1592	1757	44
force max/weight [N/kg]	24.0	25.8	25.6	25.2	25.0	26.9	12
explosive force [1/s]	12.1	13.6	14.6	17.4	18.5	18	49
SJ height [cm]	38.2	42.8	45.3	46.8	46.8	52.4	37
CMJ height [cm]	38.2	41	43.4	45.9	44.9	50.9	33
DJ24 height [cm]	33.5	36.5	37.7	40	39.8	46.3	38
DJ24 time [ms]	210	203	204	193	205	184	-12

With respect to the physical strength and power development, it is obvious that bodyweight increases more pronounced than the bodyheight within the age of 14 to 19 years. The relation of height to weight gets worse. The ability of maximal strength can be enhanced by 44%, whereas the normalized strength (force/weight) increases only by 12%. The jumping performance is improved by 35% and the ability of reactive strength enhances. Furthermore it can be detected that ski jumpers realise their jumping performance without improving the maximal strength relative to the weight. With respect to the results to the field study these development rates have to be verified.

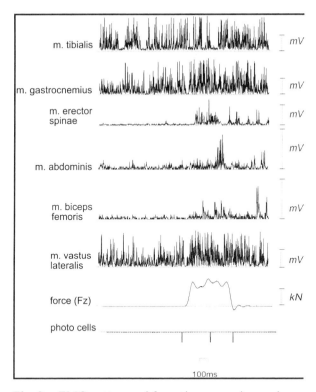

Fig. 8.   EMG-pattern and force time-curve in running-up and take-off in Ski jumping.

The comparison of the EMG pattern obtained in real ski jumping demonstrates the highly individual coordination pattern. The necessity for intra- and intermuscular coordination is obvious. For a powerful push-off, in the diagnostics of the athletes performance capability an explosive contraction type is commonly demanded. With the EMG profile demonstrated in Fig. 8 two aspects need to be pointed out: a well coordinated activation of the agonists antagonists is necessary for stabilization and optimization of the centre of gravity for push-off as well as for preparation of trunk and thigh muscles for the flight phase. The analysis of these coordination patterns, which differ between the ski jumpers, although all jumps were almost of the same performance (mean jumping distance 79,0m, mean run up velocity 87,1km/h, mean take off velocity 2,7m/s), clarify the obvious problems of a biomechanical force diagnostic on the one hand and a technical coordinated movement on the other hand.

For a differentiated performance diagnosis in ski jumping it will be necessary in future to take into account EMG patterns next to other parameters.

4.3 Cross-country-skiing: A kinematic and electromyographic analysis of the structure of the skating techniques

Since their rediscovery in the 80s skating techniques in cross-country-skiing became a discipline in the program of the FIS. These "new" techniques were not evaluated very often regarding the aspect of the movement patterns in flat terrain and the aspect of the muscular coordination.

A film analysis was done in three world cup races for a 3D-analysis of the movement patterns of the half stride skate (HSS or marathon skate) on flat terrain and the alternate stride skate (ASS or V 1) technique on moderate uphill (8°) (DLT-method, 2 cameras (35mm) synchronised, running distance 10m, 7*2*1m calibration system). Movement patterns in the HSS were analysed in 14 male and 19 female skiers. In ASS 9 male and 11 female skiers were evaluated. In addition to these measurements which were done in competition, another study regarding the muscular coordination in different techniques of cross-country-skiing was carried out in a training situation. The different movements were analysed by kinematic (3*Video, 50 Hz) and electromyographic (14 muscles) methods with 4 male athletes of the national team.

In table 2 results concerning the HSS are presented. The male skiers were faster (7,1 m/s) than the females (6,0 m/s). The cycle time of the male skiers was found to be 1,17s and for the females it was 1,09s. The partition in kick- and gliding-phase is very similar (40% to 60%). The poling time is relatively short (0,30s). With a ski angle of 15°, male skiers reach a distance between foot and track of 80cm (female: 13°, 60cm). At the end of the kick phase, the knee is not fully extended (160°). The centre of gravity (CG) is lowered by approx. 17cm while double poling.

The angle between the sole of the ski and the ground amounts at the beginning of poling -4°. This means that the outside edge of the ski touches the snow before it is posed flat. At the end of the ski thrust, an angle of 34° is reached.

Table 2. kinematic results from skis and poles in the half stride skating (marathon skate, HSS).

Parameter	unit	male (n=14)		female (n=19)	
		X	s	X	s
cycle velocity	[m/s]	**7.1**	0.3	**6.0****	0.3
cycle time	[s]	**1.17**	0.08	**1.09****	0.05
cycle rate	[1/min]	**51.3**	3.4	**55.4****	2.4
Ski-phases					
-thrust time	[s]	**0.48**	0.07	**0.43***	0.05
-gliding time	[s]	**0.69**	0.06	**0.65***	0.05
-thrust/cycle time	[%]	**40.7**	4.6	**39.1**	5.3
- gliding/cycle time	[%]	**59.3**	4.6	**60.8**	4.3
pole-phases					
-pole left	[s]	**0.27**	0.03	**0.31****	0.03
-pole left/cycle time	[%]	**23.3**	2.6	**28.7****	1.9
-pole left/thrust ski	[%]	**56.3**	7.0	**72.1****	9.2
- pole right	[s]	**0.28**	0.04	**0.32****	0.03
-pole right/cycle time	[%]	**23.4**	3.5	**29.4****	2.2
-pole right/thrust ski	[%]	**58.3**	9.6	**74.4****	10.4
* significant difference to the mean value male, p< .05.					
* * significant difference to the maen value male, p< .01.					

In ASS, the following results were found: There is only a minor shift in the CG to the side. Running speed is neither correlated with cycle length nor with cycle rate. The cycle times are the same for men and women despite a different velocity of the CG (male: 3,7m/s; female: 3,1m/s). The knee is not fully extended (160°) at the end of the kick-phase. Smaller knee angles, in combination with a high cycle rate, were present in some subjects. The gliding-phase gets shorter and the athletes used a "technique of jumping". The double poling takes place in a quite upright position of the trunk (48° to the vertical).

The EMG-study shows the following results: Each movement pattern can be described by a special coordination pattern concerning the muscular activity. (see Fig. 9) These patterns show no intraindividual and only little interindividual differences. Only short recovery phases of m. tibialis occur in ASS, especially at the end of the thrust. At this moment, the activity of m. gastrocnemius begins. The poling is more powerful and lasts 20% longer in ASS technique than in diagonal technique. Therefore, the amount of m. pectoralis activity is higher. The rate of muscle activation to the cycle time is 1/4 in diagonal technique, 1/3 in half stride skate on flat and 2/5 in alterate stride skate on moderate uphill.

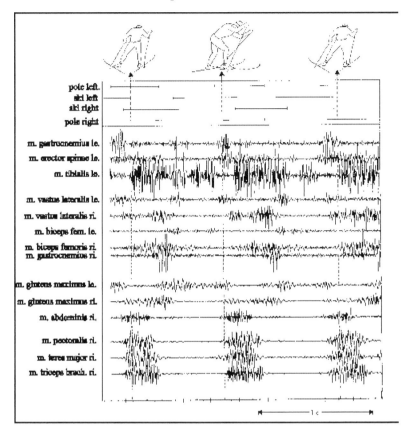

Fig. 9.   EMG-pattern of the alternate stride skate.

One of the aims of this study was to give a classification of the skating techniques. In relation to the findings of other authors and the results mentioned above, a special structure was found. By means of biomechanical criteria, depending on the movement of the skis, the arms and the pulling direction 6 different techniques of skating can be distinguished in cross-country-skiing.

5 Conclusion/Outlook

Equipment provision for biomechanical support at the OTC via cooperation with the Institute of Sports and Sportsscience of the University Freiburg is advantageous in our evaluation. Certainly, with the increase of support tasks for field measurement and courses of instruction, there repeatedly arises equipment demands which must be financed through the OTC budget.

In the future, yet stronger interdisciplinary concepts in support work must be employed. Therefore, for the area of performance diagnostics, collaboration between the Institute for Sport and Sport Science, the Department of Sports medicine at the University Clinic and the Orthopaedic Clinic in Freiburg will be further developed.

Cooperation between OTC´s has functioned well to date. Personel and equipment expense can be controlled through collaborative implementation of larger projects, for example, support in the German championships and similar venues.

All in all, the Freiburg concept of biomechanical support services has proven itself to date at the Olympic Training Centre. The principle of dividing support work among various colleagues brings great advantages in practice. Interdisciplinary translation of problems and solution initiatives is also possible. For colleagues who are involved in fundamental research, the remains a direct exchange of information, and through university connections, national and international relationships and contacts are obtained and preserved: "without basic research ..., certainly oriented towards the person and performance praxis, scientific support... could not be further developed." (G. HAGEDORN, 1987).

6 References

BÜHRLE, M.: Maximalkraft - Schnellkraft - Reaktivkraft. In: Sportwissenschaft, 3, 1989, S.311-325

GOLLHOFER, A.: Neuromuskuläre Aktivierung - Einsatzmöglichkeit im Spitzensport. NORAXON: EMG Fibel. Sportomed. Mannheim, 1993

JORGE, M.; HULL, M.L. (1986). Analysis of EMG measurement during bicycle pedalling. In:

Journal of Biomechanics. 19, 683-694.

KAUTZ, S.; FELTNER, M.E.; COYLE, E.F.; BAYLOR, A.M. (1991). The pedaling technique of elite endurance cyclists: changes with increasing workload at constant cadence. In: Int. Journal of Sport Biomechanics. 7, 29-53.

SCHWIRTZ, A./TAPKEN, S./ANDRES, U.: Diagnose - Datenbankverwaltung 3.0; IfSS Universität Freiburg, 1994

SCHWIRTZ, A.: Bewegungstechnik und muskuläre Koordination beim Skilanglauf, Köln 1994

SMITH, G.A., NELSON, R.C., FELDMAN, A., RANKINEN, J.L.: Analysis of V 1 skating technique of olympic cross-country-skiiers. In: Int. J. of Sport Biomechanics, 5, 185-207, 1989

SMITH, G.A.: Biomechanical analysis of cross-country skiing techniques. In: Medicine and Science in Sports and Exercise, 24(9), 1015-1022, 1992

TAYLOR, A.D.; BRONKS, R. (1995). Reproducibility and validity of the quadriceps muscle integrated electromygram threshold during incremental cycle ergometry. In: European Journal of Applied Physiology. 70, 252-257.

8
TESTING AND TRAINING FOR TOP NORWEGIAN ATHLETES

P. E. REFSNES
Norwegian National Sports Centre

Keywords: alpine skiing, eccentric strength, Norway, physiology, strength training, testing.

Introduction

In this paper I will provide some brief information about methods that are used in testing and training top Norwegian athletes. Naturally, this information will be general as I cannot yet give detailed information concerning unpublished test results. Likewise, I cannot give unpublished information in any detail concerning experiments with eccentric training at the National Sports Centre. This paper is not intended to be a scientific paper, but hopefully it will be relevant for athletes and coaches.

Top Norwegian athletes have competed successfully at the highest international level in both summer and winter sports in recent years. It is a common opinion among most athletes and coaches in a variety of sports that the National Sports Centre has been an important factor for this success.

A short introduction to the National Sports Centre

The Norwegian National Sports Centre (TS) is located in Oslo, close to the Norwegian University of Sport and Physical Education (NIH). The centre is owned by the Norwegian Sport Federation (NIF), and the Norwegian Olympic Committee (NOK) is responsible for the daily activities at the centre. A superior goal for the centre and for the Olympic Committee is to create optimal conditions for top Norwegian athletes so that they can train and compete at the highest international level. This has been a success, and many of the top Norwegian athletes train either regularly or for shorter periods of time at the centre. In addition some top foreign athletes use the centre too on a regular basis.

The centre includes several departments such as a department of health and medical treatment, a testing and training department, and a hotel department. In the medical department there are two doctors, three physiotherapists and one nurse working full-time, as well as a psychologist. Their main functions are directed to medical care of elite athletes. Athletes with injuries or illness are treated immediately. More serious injuries are cared for by hospitals in Oslo, especially for cases in which surgery or consultations with specialists are required.

The testing and training department deals with several problems concerning both testing and training of top athletes. There are facilities for strength training and testing as well as for endurance. As an example of the integration between different departments, two of the rooms at the hotel department are built as a high altitude chambers. Research and training in this chamber are essential to give the athletes optimal preparation before competition at high altitudes, in particular for the immediately coming years as the next winter Olympics will be held in Salt Lake City at altitudes of 1500 m and higher. There are also specific facilities for training coordination and gymnastics.

Besides optimal facilities for training and testing, specialists in areas such as endurance, strength and power, coordination, nutrition and more are connected to the centre, and most of them work there on a full-time basis. Most of those working at the centre received their education from the University for Sport and Physical Education located only 50 m from the centre, some of the staff members work half-time at the university and half-time at the centre.

The Norwegian Sports Federation is a leading force in the fight against drugs in sports; anyone training at the centre may be tested for use of illegal drugs at any time. Throughout the year the controllers arrive at least once a week. Most athletes appreciate the regular testing, feeling confident that the testing procedures are good and that the analyses will be treated securely.

The physiological basis for strength training

To compete at a high international level in most sports today, one needs high strength (both maximal-, explosive- and sub maximal strength), endurance (aerobic and anaerobic), speed, flexibility, coordination and so on. The word strength is used in many different contexts. With strength we mean the ability of muscles to develop force at a specified velocity. Increasing ones level of physical performance also increases ones possibilities to compete at a higher level in the specific sport in question. The purpose of all physical training is to stress muscles, tendons, the heart, the nervous system and so on to improve each organ's capacity. The muscles in particular have a remarkable ability to adapt as a consequence of training.

To improve muscle strength, endurance, speed and so on one must load the muscle beyond a minimum level. This is known as the principle of progressive resistance training. Since the ancient Greeks, coaches and athletes have tried to improves methods for strength training. Best known is the example of Milos from Croton. He lifted a baby bull every day. As Milos increased his strength, the training load was progressively increased when the bull grew heavier. This is a fundamental principle concerning all types of training.

A major stimulus for increasing muscular strength and hypertrophy seems to be muscle activity at forces above the levels used in daily activities. This is especially true for well-trained athletes. A review article by McDonagh and Davies (1984) seems to support this view. They concluded that loads greater than 66% of MVC (maximal voluntary isometric contraction force) are necessary to produce gains in maximal voluntary force.

The contractile characteristics of muscle is of great importance both in daily living and in sports. The development of force, and hence movement, is the result of the conversion of chemical energy to force development - mechanical work - and heat released in the muscles.

There are basically four types of muscular actions. In concentric action the muscle shortens as it develops force. The velocity of shortening can be very fast when the muscles act against no or very low load, but as the load is progressively increased, the velocity of shortening decreases. In an isometric action the load equals the maximum force, and the muscles develop force with no change in length. The relation between force and velocity is expressed by the classical force-velocity curve.

The maximum shortening velocity of an unloaded muscle depends on the proportion of fiber type. Basically, there are two main fiber types called fast fibers (Type II fibers) and slow fibers (Type I-fibers), respectively. The Type II fibers can be further divided into two subgroups called Type IIB and Type IIA fibers). Type IIB fibers are the fastest, but they fatigue easily. At the other end of the scale are Type I-fibers which are slower but more resistant to fatigue. In muscles with a high proportion of fast fibers the maximum velocity under unloaded conditions is typically 2-3 times higher than in muscles dominated by slow fibers (Close, 1972). A high proportion of fast fibers may be an advantage in sports like sprinting. For long distance runners and cross-country skiers however, the opposite is probably true.

Since muscle fiber type may be important for muscle function, a possible conversion from one type to the other has been of interest. Evidence suggests that the slow fibers cannot be transformed to fast fibers by training. Today we have evidence suggesting that the percentage of fast fibers is reduced even after strength training. Hather et. al. (1991) reported that after a period of strength training the fastest fibers (Type IIB) were almost entirely transformed to Type IIA fibers. In paralyzed muscles there is a predominance of the fastest fibers, amounting in some cases to nearly 100% (Salmons et. al, 1981). These findings are confirmed in studies with electric stimulation of isolated muscle fibers. Stimulation of fast fibers with low frequencies of impulses combined with a high number of impulses and also stimulation with a high frequencies of impulses combined with a high number of impulses have produced transformation from fast to slow muscle fiber characteristics. To transform slow muscles to fast muscle fiber characteristics, studies on rats suggest that the frequencies of impulses should be high but that the number of impulses should be low (L⁻mo et. al, 1980). If these data can be extrapolated to man, they suggest that to develop explosive muscle strength each training session should have a lower number of impulses to the muscle, that is a low training volume, but that the impulses should be given at a high frequency. The development of endurance probably depends on the training volume, that is on a high number of impulses given to the muscles during one training session. These considerations suggest that there may be a conflict between an optimal training of endurance and explosive strength.

However, the maximum shortening velocity of an unloaded muscle is also proportional to the length of the muscle. When the muscle length is increased by increasing the number of sarcomeres in series, the maximum shortening velocity will increase proportionally to the change in length. The muscle length is easily increased by stretching exercises. Good flexibility, especially in the hip joint, is also required to optimize the lifting technique in some exercises. Thus, there are probably several reasons to include training of flexibility.

Increased strength by training is explained both as a result of hypertrophy (increased CSA) and also of neural adaptation. It has been shown that the maximum isometric force correlates well with the physiological cross-sectional area (CSA) of the muscles (Chapman et. al. 1984). A study by Ikai and Fukunaga (1970) showed on the other hand little correlation between increased strength and increase in crossectional area. Thus, neural adaptation was probably important in that study. If a muscle increases its force gradually, more and more fibers are recruited according to Henneman's size principles. First small motor units involving Type I fibers are engaged. As the force increases, larger motor units involving Type IIA fibers are also engaged. To develop a maximum force, the Type IIB fibers must also be engaged. It may well be that an untrained person may not be able to recruit the fastest fibers with the highest recruitment threshold, that is Type IIB fibers. As a result of training the formerly untrained subject may then be able to fully activate Type IIB fibers also and thus increase his maximum force. It can be very difficult to separate the effects of neural adaptation from structural changes. It is conceivable that in the early phases of training or when a new type of exercise is introduced, neural adaptations probably dominate. This is in accordance with the results reported by Ikai and Fukunaga (1970). They found that isometric strength increased by 90-100% and that the cross-sectional area increased by only 20%. As training continues, neural adaptation probably becomes fully exploited. Further development of the contractile properties of the muscle, leading to hypertrophy, then becomes more and more important.

When the load exceeds the muscle force, muscles lengthen as they develop force in eccentric action. The force generated during eccentric action increases with increasing velocity of lengthening, reaching a value of about 1.8 times the isometric force (Jones and Round - 1990). Seliger et al. (1980) found that the force was almost three times greater during eccentric action in squat than during concentric action and that maximum isometric force tended to approach that of concentric action.

But natural movements seldom occur as purely concentric, isometric or eccentric actions. Normally, muscles are stretched (eccentric action) immediately before shortening (concentric action). This muscle action is referred to as the stretch-shortening cycle (SSC), sometimes described as plyometrics action. The origin of the word is derived from the Greek word *pleythyein* and means to increase. Under this condition, energy is absorbed by the muscles in the eccentric phase and stored as elastic potential energy in the elastic elements in series with the contractile filaments. This energy is partially used to increase mechanical power output in the concentric phase, provided there is short coupling time - the time delay between the stretching phase and shortening phase (Cavagna et. al. 1968), while some of the stored elastic energy is lost as heat. This means that in a plyometric action, the force-velocity curve is shifted to the right in the concentric phase of action. However, the increased power output may also be explained by an increased reflex potentiation in a plyometric action.

Traditionally top athletes did not include eccentric training regularly, but the reason for this is not known. Eccentric actions are physiologically normal in all movements, especially in sports. In several studies suggest that the muscular strength increases more after eccentric training than in other types of training (Komi and Buskirk, 1972, Colliander and Tesch, 1990 and Dudley et al., 1991), and eccentric training also seems to lead to greater hypertrophy (Komi and Buskirk - 1972 and Hather et al. - 1991) than traditionally strength training. Accordingly, eccentric training should be considered as the most efficient of various strength training regimes.

Development of optimal muscle strength is of crucial importance in most athletic performance, and strength training has therefore become a supplement to conventional training for many top athletes. In weightlifting and power lifting the development of high force in a short time is important (maximum strength). In cross-country skiing and long distance running muscles must be able to develop force for a much longer period of time, but the force needed is much lower (sub maximum strength). Finally, in a high jump or long jump the muscles must create the highest possible force in the shortest possible time (explosive strength).

Leg and hip strength are regarded as major factors in the performance of most athletic activities. The full squat (that is when the surface of the thigh, at the hip joint, is lower than the highest point at the knee) must be considered to be a basis exercise for training these muscle groups.

Testing muscular strength

Explosive strength: Normally explosive strength, which is important in many sports, is tested as jumping height in a vertical jump on a force platform. Alternatively it can be tested in a horizontal jump (standing triple jump or standing long jump). Standard procedure on the platform includes standing jump (SJ) and counter movement jump (CMJ). These methods have been published elsewhere (Bosco and Komi - 1980). In the ergojump, which is described by Bosco and Komi, the jumping height is calculated from the fly-time. To secure a correct jumping height on the ergojump, the body position should be identical in landing and take-off. On our platform (Amti), the force development in the jump is used to calculate the jumping height. That means that the body position in the landing does not influence the calculated height of the jump, and we regard this is a better method for measuring jumping height, especially when jumps with extra load on the shoulder are introduced.

Standing jumps start from a position in which the knee-angle is about 90° and where no preparatory counter movement is allowed. Counter movement jumps start from a standing position, and a rapid counter movement to a position where the knee-angle is about 90° is allowed immediately followed by the vertical jump. In both standing and counter movement jumps the hands are kept on the hips throughout the jump to secure that they are performed primarily through the leg extensor muscles.

The vertical force curve for a squat jump and a counter movement jump are shown in Fig. 1. In this specific squat jump the jumping height was 52.4 cm, the peak force 2221 N, the time to reach 90% of peak force was 0.225 s, and the average force during the jump was 1682 N. The corresponding data for the counter movement jump are 55.4 cm, 2579 N, 0.128 s and 1922 N respectively.

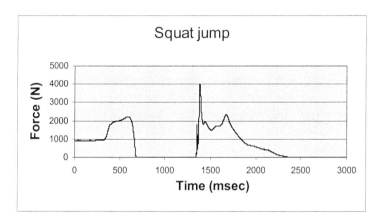

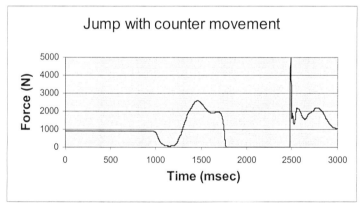

Fig. 1. The vertical force against the ground in SJ and CMJ. SJ is initiated on a signal from the tester when the athletes stands quite still, then the vertical force is equal to the body weight. In the jump, the force increases to a peak level of 2221 N, and decreases to zero by time of take-off. The peak force development about 0.6 sec after take-off, indicates the landing. In CMJ the vertical force decreases almost to zero in the counter movement before reaching the peak level (2579 N) in the jump.

In the standing jump the muscle action is purely concentric. We have found that under this condition the jumping height depends on the proportion of fiber type, and this observation agrees with prior studies (Bosco and Komi, 1979). Athletes with a high proportion of Type II fibers (> 60%) were normally better in the vertical jump than athletes with less than 40% of fast fibers, especially in the standing jump.

If jumping height for standing jumps and the counter movement jumps are compared, higher performance is naturally obtained in the counter movement jumps, possibly because of use of elastic energy stored in the eccentric phase of action. Normally the jumping height is 2-5 cm higher in counter movement jumps than in standing jumps. However, in a few cases, particularly for young athletes, we have seen some who have better results in the standing jump than in the counter movement jumps. The reason may be poor coordination, disabling the subjects from drawing advantage from the counter movement. Komi (1984) however, found that runners (800-1800 m) had the lowest difference (5 cm) between counter movement and standing jumps while ski jumpers showed the greatest difference (8-11 cm). This agrees with the Bosco's findings (1990).

We have found much less difference between the scores in counter movement and standing jumps among top Norwegian athletes compared to the results reported by Bosco (1990) and Komi (1984). These results may indicate that some top Norwegian athletes should train more for specifically explosive strength.

The standing jump can also be performed with an extra load on the shoulder, and we do that using loads of 50% (SJ 50) and 100% (SJ 100) of the body mass, to obtain more information about each individual's strength. Then the relation between explosive power and strength (F/V) can be calculated according to the formula:

$$FV\% \ = \ (SJ50/SJ) * 100 \% \ \ or \ \ (SJ100/SJ) * 100 \%$$

Imaging the following results:

SJ = (40 cm), SJ 50 = (20 cm) and SJ 100 = (10 cm).

Then: FV50 = (20 cm/40 cm) * 100% = 50%
and   FV100 = (10 cm/40 cm) * 100% = 25%.

Our experience suggests that optimal scores are about 60-65% and 35-40% for the FV50 and FV100, respectively, since these values seem to secure a good balance between explosive power and strength. This is consistent with findings by Bosco (1990). He found that FV100 was higher than 35% for many male Italian track and field athletes except for the long distance runner.

A lower relation indicates a lack of strength while a higher relation, which is very rare, would mean a need for more explosive training. The jumping test is frequently used by many top athletes in different sports, and the test results show clearly that many top Norwegian athletes must increase their maximum strength in the first instance; later they can give explosive strength training higher priority. Veroshanski and Chernousov (1974) suggest that 1RM in squat should be twice the body weight before doing explosive training. Valik (1966) and McFarlane (1982) have an opposite viewpoint and recommend explosive training before future strength training.

Our data suggest that training for maximum strength leads to a higher performance in the standing jump, especially for athletes with poor strength. To increase the performance in counter movement jumps, one must do specific explosive training in addition to the strength training.

For well-trained athletes however, we have found no relation between increased strength and increased jumping height. Our experience suggests that high-velocity training (explosive training) and low-velocity training (maximum strength training) performed at the same time is not the most effective way of training. Dietmar Schmidtbleicher has stated that for training periods of similar length, a phase of hypertrophy training followed by explosive strength training shows better results than mixed method training of the conventional type over the same period of time.

Maximum strength is commonly tested as 1RM - the highest load that can be lifted once, as maximum isometric force in a predetermined position, and as maximum eccentric force development in different exercises. Both isometric and eccentric tests are performed on a force platform.

For many years, 1RM in full squat has been a basic exercise for testing maximum strength for the leg and the hip extensors among top Norwegian athletes. In some sports a minimum level of performance is defined to assure sufficient strength. In alpine skiing for example, the minimum level is set at 2.5 times their own body mass for men and 2.2 times body mass for women in the deep squat lift. At their best, all male Norwegian skiers of the Europe and World Cup teams satisfy this criterion; in fact, some of the athletes are close to lifting 3.0 times their own body mass. Some alpine ski-trainers have suggested 3.0 times the body mass as the minimal level. In ice hockey, the level is set to (body mass + 100 kg) in the deep squat and to (body mass + 35 kg) in the bench press.

The maximum isometric force is tested in a power rack that has two sets of pins that can be adjusted to a predetermined position. The distance between the two pins is equal to the diameter of the barbell. The lower pins support the bar, while the upper pins act as stoppers for the bar. The test is done in different exercises and in different positions. Normally this test is used by powerlifters and weight lifters to find the weakest position sticking point in a range of motion (ROM) and have led to practical implications concerning training. If a power lifter is found to be weak in the lower part in a bench press, training of the pectoralis major is given high priority. If on the other hand he is found to be weak in the higher parts of the lift, training of his triceps and shoulder muscles are given higher priority.

Fig. 2 shows the maximum isometric force developed in the deepest position in squat. The athletes initiates the isometric action on signal. In this specific lift, the maximum isometric force was 2276 N (232.1 kg) and the time to reach 90% of maximal force was 1.392 s. The recording lasts for 6 s.

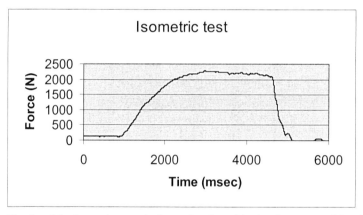

Fig. 2.   Maximum isometric force developed in the deepest position in squat.

The maximal eccentric force test is relatively new, but today we do this kind of testing on the force platform, especially for the squat lift. This is done by finding the highest load that can be lifted once from an upright position to the deepest position in squat. The lift is accepted when the velocity in the eccentric phase is constant (i.e. constant force in a full ROM) and the duration is longer than 3.5 s. The velocity of lengthening is rather slow. According to the force-velocity relation, a higher eccentric force would be expected if the speed of lengthening was higher. It should be noted that the speed of lengthening is even slower when weight lifters do eccentric training.

An example of the force generation is given in Fig. 3. In this specific lift the load was 300 kg, and it is clear that the vertical force is relatively constant during the whole range of motion. However, the mean calculated force was 2916 N (297.3 kg), and the duration was 4.10 s. According to our criteria a lift is not accepted if the force level drops below 97% of the average force before the bar hits the rack. The curve in question in Fig. 3 shows a definite drop in force immediately before that point. The reason is that one side of the bar hits the rack a little bit earlier than the other side, and this may also explain why the average force is actually a little bit lower than the actual load.

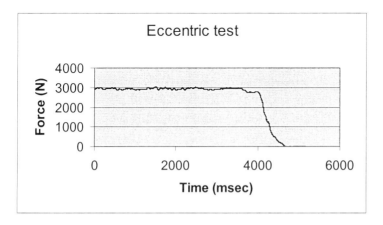

Fig. 3. Maximum eccentric force curve in a deep squat. Force recording starts immediately after the initiation of the eccentric phase and lasts for 6 s.

The curves that are shown in this paper are all from a young Norwegian track and field athlete who has been engaged in strength training for a long time. His body mass is 93 kg, and his personal best in a deep squat is 230 kg. As we see from the results, his isometric strength in the lowest position in the squat is just a little bit higher (232.1 kg). His eccentric force development is, however, about 30% higher than his 1RM test. This is higher than expected on his level of performance, but his strength profile is consistent with findings by Seliger (1980). His results on the explosive tests are also excellent, probably because of his unique strength and possibly also due to genetic factors.

Normally, submaximal strength is tested as the maximal number of repetitions in an exercise with a load corresponding to 70% of 1RM. However, some top athletes, for example rowers, use loads up to 80% of maximum on this test. Others, for example sailors, use a load corresponding to 60% of 1RM. The number of repetitions gives a good expression of submaximal strength. Normally we expect about 15-20 repetitions on a load of 70% of 1RM. For subjects being well below this level we suggest that submaximal training should be given higher priority. If on the other hand the subject does considerably more than 20 repetitions, maximal strength training is given highest priority. Two alpine skiers with a 1RM in squat of 200 kg, did nine and 30 repetitions respectively of 140 kg. Consequently, the strength training program for these two athletes was changed accordingly and is no longer identical.

Submaximal strength differs for different sports. Sprinters in speed skating perform between 10-15 repetitions on the sub-maximum test, alpine skiers between 20-25 and long distance speedsters usually do more than 30 repetitions. However, 1RM and explosive power levels are much higher for alpine skiers and sprinters than for long distance skaters. This is easily explained due to higher body mass and cross-sectional area for sprinters and alpine skiers and probably also because of a higher proportion of fast fibers. A higher proportion of slow fibers would probably give a higher score on the submaximal test.

Training (eccentric training)

We have done several studies on the effect of eccentric training that have not yet been published. Central for these studies are adequate equipment. Since little commercial equipment was available, we have designed and built our own equipment for eccentric training at load well above 1RM.

The systems are mechanically very simple. An external load, consisting in fact of two separate components, is in direct connection with a bar. In training, the athletes are lowering both the bar and the external load. In a predetermined position, part of the external load is automatically released. Thereafter the subject lifts the reduced load (bar and reduced external load) to the standing position. The released external load is automatically lifted to the start position by a piston before being coupled to the system. In this system, a higher load is therefore used in the eccentric phase of a lift than in the concentric.

We have built several systems for eccentric training designed for elbow flexion, bench press, and squat respectively. The systems are used in training experiments and in the daily training of many top Norwegian athletes. In particular ice hockey players, alpine skiers, track and field athletes, powerlifters, and weight lifter among others use the systems regularly. Even cross-country skiers have used the squat machine periodically in off-season training. Top foreign athletes have also used the systems at the elite athlete centre as well. Lately some of the best weight lifters in the world from the former Soviet union have tried it, and a similar system is built in Stockholm for top Swedish athletes.

Eccentric training is extremely hard and can be dangerous. One can of course do eccentric training by overloading the weights in traditionally free weight training, and thereupon get help in the concentric phase. But it has a few disadvantages. Naturally one must train with weights that are heavier than those one can handle alone, and therefore it requires help from a training partner. The partner, however, should be properly trained so that he can spot the athlete safely whatever happens. In the squat, for instance, a tremendous load is put on the partner. Eccentric training can also be done on ordinary strength training machines for leg extension, leg curl, bench press etc. One can for example lower weights in the eccentric phase with one leg or arm, and use both legs or arms in the concentric phase.

We do not recommend athletes starting eccentric training too early. A minimum requirement is that they are well familiar with traditional strength training and have reached a specific strength minimum before they are introduced to eccentric training. The moral is that 'one should learn to crawl before walking'. Thus, eccentric training is not recommended for younger athletes. We are especially afraid of injuries of the tendons and ligaments since these structures do not adapt to strength training as fast as muscles. A former Olympic 10,000 m runner (Jeff Galloway) once said that „the single greatest cause of improvement is remaining injury-free". We agree, one can have the best trainer in the world, the best training program as well, it is worth nothing if one gets seriously injured. As a conclusion, eccentric training can be compared to high altitude training: It is used primarily for top athletes who have trained for years.

In recent years we have done several training studies with eccentric training, and we have also received much information from top athletes who have regularly trained eccentrically. It is a common experience that strength training leads to tremendous muscle soreness, referred to as 'delayed onset muscle soreness' (muscle soreness that appears 24 to 48 h after a hard workout) and unpleasant sensation. This is especially the case when introducing new exercises to a program, and in previous studies it is well documented that this muscle soreness and temporarily reduced force generation is associated with eccentric training. As the training continues, muscles adapt to this training, and muscle soreness will diminish.

Newham et. al. (1987) reported a 50% decrease in MVC after one bout of extreme eccentric training, and MVC was significantly lower even 14 days later. Our experience is that the restitution process is much faster for top athletes. A few athletes performed better both on jumping tests (SJ and CMJ) and on the maximum isometric test 24 h after an extremely hard eccentric training session. This is very rare, however, and we recommend a longer recovery period for most athletes. Normally we recommend eccentric training once or twice a week for top athletes. One of the most successfully Norwegian female powerlifters (Beate Amdahl), with a body mass at the time of 60 kg, trained eccentrically once a week for 2 years. She always lifted three sets with three repetitions in both the squat and bench press. Her 1RM in squat increased from 180 kg to 210 kg during this period, and this is still the world record for her body mass. She is convinced that eccentric training was important for her success. It is also worth mentioning that Beate, and also two other female powerlifters, have some of the best test results ever on the vertical jumping test at the elite Norwegian athlete centre. The same tendency is also clear for male powerlifters. Two of them are among the best ever tested on the SJ and CMJ, and both of them were among the best powerlifters in the world.

The literature quotes scientists and coaches recommending training loads at 100-180% of 1RM for eccentric training. We have experienced that well-trained athletes tolerate a lower eccentric load relative to their 1RM than untrained athletes. World class elite powerlifters use loads no more than 105-110% of their 1RM in squat lift and bench press, whilst athletes on a lower level can use loads up to 120-130% of 1RM. In a test, the men's alpine skiing European Cup team performed 1.19 times the 1RM in eccentric squat. In other exercises however, such as elbow flexion, the loads can be higher (130-180 % of 1RM), but it is still the case that well-trained athletes use a lower eccentric load than untrained athletes. It is difficult to give the exact load, but the load should be high enough that the working muscles are stretched despite maximum effort to avoid stretching.

In eccentric training the athletes are instructed to use 3-6 s in the eccentric phase. Their entire concentration should be focused on decelerating the load. When the velocity in the eccentric phase becomes too fast, one should stop the training or reduce the load. Earlier, when our knowledge about eccentric training was poor, we also used a high eccentric load followed by a high concentric load (up to 80-90% of 1RM). This was mentally very hard, and concentration was focused on the concentric phase since this phase seemed to be the hardest. In a later experiment we have found that it is the eccentric loading and not the concentric load that is important for increasing muscular strength and hypertrophy. Today we still use a very high load in the eccentric phase, but not more than 50% of 1RM for the concentric phase.

In training experiments we usually test maximum strength (as 1RM, MVC, or maximal eccentric force), explosive strength (as SJ and CMJ), and cross-sectional area by using CT images (computer tomography). We conclude that strength, the cross-sectional area of the muscles, and power increase significantly more after eccentric training than after traditional isometric or concentric training. Even top athletes who have carried out hard traditional strength training for years show a considerable further increase in strength and muscle hypertrophy when they include eccentric training in their regular training programs.

We have found that traditional training with free weights leads to significant increases of 1RM and CSA, but no changes in SJ and CMJ. In one experiment we found that well-trained athletes who trained with weights in the traditional manner tended to decrease (not significantly statistically) in their performance of standing jumps, counter movement jumps, and drop jumps (DJ). This is consistent with findings by Häkkinen et al. (1985) who concluded that heavy resistance weight training caused primarily an increase in isometric force, whilst explosive jump training led to an increase in isometric rate of force development (RFD). The reason could be that the explosive jump training caused a specific increase in the rate of motor unit activation onset, but this adaptation was not found after high resistance weight training.

In our experiments with eccentric training we have also found a significant increase in standing jump and counter movement jump scores. Some coaches recommend slow eccentric training only in a preparation period, because this training is associated with decreased RFD. There are indications, however, that the fastest fibers are preferentially recruited in the eccentric phase (Nardone et. al. 1989). The selective activation of the fastest fibers was however most pronounced in fast eccentric actions.

This accords with our results in a case study of a national caliber bodybuilder. We found an increased proportion of Type II B fibers after 8 weeks of plyometric training of the elbow flexors. He trained the elbow flexion in a way that can be compared to a drop jump. A load of 30% of 1RM was released and fell freely for 60 cm before causing a very rapid but short stretching of the maximally isometrically activated elbow flexors immediately followed by a concentric action. Before this training, the athlete had no fibers classified as Type IIB, but after the training period we found several Type IIB fibers. This may perhaps be explained as a selective recruitment of the fastest fibers during the extremely explosive training, and these results may indicate that training can convert other fibers to Type IIB fibers.

In some sports eccentric force generation will be particularly high, for example for musculature of the quadriceps in alpine skiing (Berg et. al. 1995). It may therefore be important to improve the maximal eccentric force in particular. We have found that after a period with eccentric training the increase in athletes' maximal eccentric force is significantly higher than increase in their 1RM. In traditional weight training using the same load in eccentric and concentric phases, the eccentric force generation is far from maximal, and there is no optimal stress on the working muscles in the eccentric phase. To achieve this, one must load the muscles in the eccentric phase by more than a 1RM load. Eccentric training is therefore strongly recommended for alpine skiers, for example.

Its obvious that there is also a psychological effect in eccentric training. When one gets used to training with weights that are much higher than one's initial 1RM, that weight will be found easy to handle after a period of eccentric training.

The results of our studies have led to changes in the training regimes of top Norwegian athletes. We regard eccentric training to be an excellent way to overload the muscles and many top athletes use eccentric training regularly in their strength and power training. In the future we assume that this type of training will be regarded as necessary for many groups of athletes. Even a manufacturer of commercial strength training equipment, the American Life Fitness company for instance, has built machines that are based on the principle of plyometric training, and these machines are used by people who are not engaged in top-level athletics.

We think that maximal strength is necessary also for improvement of the explosive strength. Many top athletes engaged in sports that require excellent explosive strength have neglected training of their maximal strength and have had to pay the price for this. When their motor is too small, they have by no means the same potential for increasing their performance, even with proper explosive strength training.

References

1. Berg, H., Eiken, O. And Tesch, P. A. Involvement of eccentric muscle actions in giant slalom racing. Med. Sci. Sports Exerc. Vol. 27, no. 12, pp 1666-1670, 1995.
2. Bosco, C., and Komi, P. V. Mechanical characteristics and fiber composition of human leg extensors muscle. Eur. J. Appl. Physiol. 41:280, 1979.

3. Bosco, C., and Komi, P. V. Influence of Aging on the mechanical behaviour of the leg extensors muscles. Eur. J. Appl. Physiol. 45:209-219, 1980.

4. Bosco, C. New test for training control of athletes. *Techniques in Athletics*, Cologne 7-9 June 1990.

5. Cavagna, G. A., Dusman, B. and Margaria, R. Positive work done by a previously stretched muscle. J. Appl. Physiol. 24(1): 21-32, 1968.

6. Chapman, S. J., Grindrod, S. R. and Jones, D. A. Cross-sectional area and force production of quadriceps muscle. J. Physiol. 353:53P, 1984.

7. Close, R. I. Dynamic properties of mammalian skeletal muscles. Physiol. Rew. 52:129-197, 1972.

8. Colliander, E. B. and Tesch, P. A. Effects of eccentric and concentric muscle actions in resistance training. Acta Physiol Scand 140, 31-39, 1990.

9. Häkkinen, K., Alen, M. and Komi. P. V. Changes in isometric force- and relaxation-time, electromyographic and muscle fiber characteristics of human skeletal muscle during strength training and detraining. Acta Physiologica Scandinavica , 125, 573-85, 1985.

10. Häkkinen, K., Komi. P. V and Alen, M. Effect of explosive type strength training on isometric force- and relaxation-time, electromyographic and muscle fiber characteristics of leg extensor muscles. Acta Physiologica Scandinavica , 125, 587-600, 1985.

11. Hather, B. M., Tesch, P. A., Buchanan, P. and Dudley, G. A. Influence of eccentric actions on skeletal muscle adaptions to resistance training. Acta. Physiol. Scand. 143:177-185, 1991.

12. Ikai, M and Fukunaga, T. A study on training effect on strength per unit cross-sectional area of muscle by means of ultrasonic measurements. Int. Z. Angew. Physiol. 28:173-180, 1970.

13. Jones, D. A. and Round, J. M. Skeletal muscle in health and disease. A textbook of muscle physiology. Manchester university press, Manchester, England (1990).

14. Komi, P. V. Physiological and biomechanical correlates of muscle function: Effects of muscle structure and stretch-shortening cycle on force and speed. Exer. Sport. Sci. Rew. 12:81-121, 1984.

15. Komi, P. and Buskirk, E. R. Effect of eccentric and concentric muscle conditioning on tension and electrical activity of human muscle. Ergonomics, vol. 15, no. 4, 417-434, 1972.

16. Lömo, T., Westgaard, R. H. and Engebretsen, L. Different stimulation patterns affect contractile properties of denervated rat soleus muscles. Plasticity of Muscles. Walter de Gruyter & Co., Berlin-New York, 1980.

17. Nardone, A., Romano, C. and Schieppati, M. Selective recruitment of high-threshold human motor-units during voluntary isotonic lengthening of active muscles. Journal of Physiology, 409, 451-471, 1989.

18. Newham, D. J., Jones, D. A. and Clarkson, P. M. Repeated high-force eccentric exercise: effects on muscle pain and damage. J. Appl. Physiol. 63(4):1381-1386, 1987.

19. McFarlane, B. Jumping exercises. Track & Field Quarterly Review. 82(4), 54-55, 1982.

20. Salmons, S. and Henriksson, J. Muscle & Nerve, vol. 4:94-105, 1981.

21. Seliger, V., Dolejs, L. and Karas, V. A Dynamometric Comparison of Maximum Eccentric, Concentric and Isometric Contractions using EMG and Energy Expenditure Measurements. Eur J Appl Physiol 45, 235-244 (1980).

22. Valik, B. Strength preparation of young track and fielders. Physical culture in school, 4:28, 1966.

23. Veroshanski, Y. and Chernousov, G. Jumps in the training of a sprinter. Track and Field, 9:16, 1974.

9
SCIENCE IN ELITE SPORT

J. ESCODA
Director of Sport Sciences. R&D Manager
CAR, Sant Cugat, Barcelona, Spain

Keywords: biomechanics, CAR, organization, physiology, research, running, Spain, swimming, tennis.

An integral training and education proposal

Sport science is part of our common scope and to make it useful in a systematic way is daily even a more difficult task.

In our short experience in the field of sports sciences application, our center is ten years of age, which is not a long time at all but enough to take into account previous experiences in eastern and western countries, which has stimulated our developing something we have understood as a new idea in our field.

Basically based on an equilibrium between facilities, technical, academic, health and research support to coaches and athletes, in 1987 we started promoting the concept we called *integral preparation* for elite athletes.

In the favorable environment of the Barcelona '92 Olympic nomination, the Olympic Training Center of Barcelona (also called CAR, Centre d'Alt Rendiment) located in Sant Cugat, a privileged residential area next to Barcelona, started to work.

CAR was established to tend to the preparation of future Olympic athletes of the entire country and became increasingly a stopping point of many Olympic teams of the world.

Founded as a public company, it is supported by the Catalan Government and also by the Spanish Sports Council

A Public Company created to provide athletes with all the facilities, human, technical and scientific resources to reach the highest sports levels.
D.O.G. Feb. 3rd, 1989

The governing bodies are composed by members from the Catalonian and Spanish government.

°GENERAL BOARD

President: President of Generalitat of Catalonia
1st Vicepresident : Minister of Sports (SPAIN)
2nd VP:Minister of Sports (CATALONIA)
3rd VP: General Director of Sports of the National Sports Council

Members : 3 from Generalitat of Catalonia
3 from National Sports Council

°ADMINISTRATION BOARD

President: Catalonia Secretariat of Sports

Members:
General Director of Sports
General Director of Education Centers
Assistant Director of Health
Assistant Director of President's affaires
Director of Physical Education Institut
Director of CAR

CAR is designed to provide integral support for athletes' preparation and has been organized by operating units covering a wide range of services: Academic, sports, health care, sports science and administrational units take care of the daily needs of permanent or visiting athletes.

Hierarchy of priorities

Based on the concept of attending to the overall needs of an athlete as to guarantee full preparation, we have arranged priorities as follows.

This is based on the following requirements:
1. The need for high volume and quality training
2. The need for preservation of health
3. The need for integral training

Priorities to meet the described requirements are established. The first priority is related to the main task developed by the athlete which is training. Facilities and equipment thus comprise the aspect covered at the first level. Following that, academic preparation is covered. A sports career is only part of the person's life. Thus a future for a life without sports competition must be guaranteed.

The next level is health: We must assume that high performance means high risk, and health is a mandatory issue of attention. Finally, performance must be measured and analyzed providing tools to guarantee scientific training for coaches and athletes.

The following figure represents the work flow of the integral training process not only where the athlete's activity is focused in their sports performance as a short term goal, but also on her or his future, which will be their life after the period of high performance.

WORKFLOW INTEGRAL TRAINING

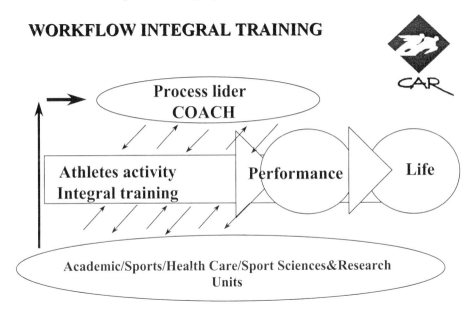

Notice the interactivity between athletes, various units and most obviously with the coach, who as our process leader also receives feedback from these units, who acts in consequence as the closest relation to the athlete in daily work, as a father, brother and friend.

Organization

How is it organized?

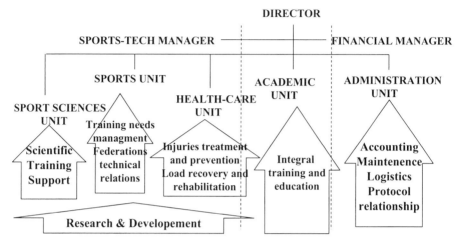

Our organization described below is composed of 5 operating units covering the previously mentioned complementary priorities.

Academic Unit. This unit cares for the athletes' schooling and provides tutorials during their stay at the center. An official Institute within the center provides regular studies adapted to training schedules

Sports Unit. This unit provides facilities and equipment to coaches and athletes.

Health Unit. Externally linked to a central hospital, this unit provides assistance ranging from first aid to rehabilitation and training recovery.

The Sports Sciences Unit provides support in physiology, psychology, biomechanics and coaches' advising, the management of multidisciplinary projects in research and development.

Administrational Unit. The center, as a public company requires administration. This unit provides financial supporters and customer management.

A wide range of services are being provided by the units, from residence to sports facilities, from schooling to health care, sports science and research.

The services described as follows in the various Units and Departments and can be supplied on demand for permanent athletes and for external Federations and Sport Clubs with elite athletes.

Residence

- 325 beds in double rooms and quad rooms with bath (TV + Phone)
- Bungalows with 8 and 12 beds
- Full and half meal plans
- Stand-alone services: Breakfast - Lunch - Dinner

Facilities

The CAR Olympic Training Center has specialized facilities for the following sports:

- 3 fitness rooms
- Track and field (all events)
- Swimming (2 heated indoor and outdoor)
- Tennis (Synthetic floor)
- Table tennis
- Weightlifting
- Taekwondo
- Wrestling
- Judo
- Gymnastics
- Basketball
- Handball
- Volleyball
- Roller Hockey
- Badminton
- Soccer

Health & Sport Science Medicine

- Basic health examinations
- Medical checkup
- Basic blood analysis
- Special requirements (Blood analysis)
- Special test
- Drugs
- Traumatological checkup

- Specialist checkup
- Radiography
- Ecography
- Ecocardiography
- Gamagraphy
- Magnetic Resonance Scan

Services

HEALTH CARE

Medicine and Sports Medicine

Traumatology and Orthopedics

Imaging diagnosis

Blood analysis

Physiotherapy

Chiropody

Optometrics

•**HOSPITAL TERRASSA**

Podiatry

- Podiatric checkup
- Podiatric study
- Personalized Computerized Inserts

Physiotherapy

- Manual treatment
- Massage
- Recuperation massage
- Muscle stretching

- Diadynamics
- Interferencials
- Iontophoresis
- Electrostimulation
- T.N.S.
- Microwaves
- Ultrasound
- Infrared
- Functional bandage
- Paraffin Baths
- Contrast Baths
- Cryotherapy
- R.P.G. Treatment
- Manual Hydrotherapeutic Treatment
- SPA - Jacuzzi
- Sauna
- Electrotherapy
- Laser therapy
- Magnetotherapy

Optometry

- Basic optometric test
- Specialized optometric test
- Full optometric test
- (ACU-VISION)

Planning and Support

- Planning computerization
- Technical documentation
- Planning intervention
- Individual planning consulting
- Group planning consulting
- Fitness test
- Teledocumentation - CD-ROM SPORT-DISCUS

Physiology

- Kineanthropometry
- VO2 max test
- Lactate test
- Ph test
- Field test
- Blood analysis for training control
- Special requirements (Blood analysis)
- Dynamometric test (CYBEX)
- Pulse meter SPORTESTER
- Flexibility test
- Height prediction
- Body Composition with MRI
- Metabolic study with MRS

Services

SPORTS SCIENCES

PHYSIOLOGY AND FUNCTIONAL EVALUATION

VO2 max

Kinanthropometry (MRI SSR)

Dynamometry (CYBEX)

Lab analysis (Lactate,pH,Urea)

Field test

**Nutrition: Individual Support
Quality control**

Nutrition

- Dietetic checkup
- Computerized nutritional study
- Special menu design

Psychology

- Psychological test
- Individual session
- Group session
- 1st Interview
- Advising session

Biomechanics

- 2D recording session
- 3D recording session
- Bidimensional study using the CAR System
- Bidimensional study using PEAK PERFORMANCE
- Three dimensional study using PEAK PERFORMANCE
- COMPAMM-SPORT 3D visualization
- COMPAMM-SPORT Kinematics and dynamics study
- COMPAMM-SPORT Simulation
- COMPAMM-SPORT for TV Broadcast
- CAR software package for W95
- Photocells TAG-HEUER IND
- Photocells TAG-HEUER GROUP
- KISTLER Force platform analysis IND
- KISTLER Force platform analysis GROUP
- EMG study NORAXON IND
- EMG study NORAXON GROUP

Services

SPORTS SCIENCES

BIOMECHANICS

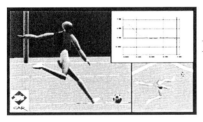

Kinematic analysis:
Photocells
Videography

Forces analysis:
Force plates

3D Visualization:
DMC
Compamm-Sport
Alias-Wavefront

Research & Development

- Specific research projects

Sport Science Applications

The various departments of the Sport Sciences Unit in conjunction with coaches' programs systematically develop and administer applied performance tests to athletes as explained below.

Sport Sciences Applications

SWIMMING

PHYSIOLOGY AND BIOMECHANICS

Stroke and Turns video analysis
Flexibility test with video
Lactate test

Swimming. A multidisciplinary test is performed periodically by swimmers using different protocols, some of which are developed here, others adapted. These include biomechanical analysis of starting and stroke analysis using videography, a progressive lactate test, anthropometric evaluation and flexibility test using videography.

Sport Sciences Applications

MIDDLE AND LONG DISTANCE RUNNERS

PHYSIOLOGY AND PLANNING

Léger & Boucher protocol
Borsetto et col. protocol
Lactate test
Multimedia supported

Track and Field. A specially adapted progressive lactate test with multimedia support for middle distance runners is performed in the training program.

Race Walking. Simulated competitions are performed on the treadmill with psychological support preceding the most important events during the season.

Tennis and Table Tennis. Specially developed psychological support programs are provided for these racket sports.

Pushing research to the top

Research and Development, both public and private, is part of the activity performed in various international programs at CAR providing resources and expertise in research to the departments' members and to the center.

Research & Development

MARES Project
Muscle Atrophy Research and Exercise System
Supported by NASA & ESA

NTE and CAR develops together and ergometer for astronauts to be used in the International Space Laboratory ALPHA

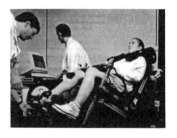

A research project supported by the European Space Agency now performed at CAR involves advising an engineering company in the development of an ergometer for use by astronauts in the future International Space Lab, ALPHA. This device is to evaluate and mitigate muscle atrophy provoked by the effects of space weightlessness; human adapters, software and engine are being developed in a multidisciplinary research team.

Research & Development

GEST Project
TV commentators support system

Supported by C+ France

Applied in 1992 and 1996 Barcelona and Atlanta Olympic Games

A development project to provide biomechanical analysis to support TV commentators at major events has been undertaken with good results in the Barcelona '92 and Atlanta '96 Olympic Games.

Other research projects in the field of nutrition are supported by private companies.

Research & Development

DTL Project
Long Jump Technology Development

Supported by I.O.C. and ONCE

New porposals for the touchdown zone

A research study sponsored by the IOC and Spanish blind association ONCE is being carried out at CAR in order to find develop new proposals for the landing zone for the long jump event.

Resources from various projects allow the center to maintain daily operation and supplement public funding, which is never enough.

Coaches' and scientists' commitment to progress

Any work done by any good scientist is unprofitable without a real life commitment by coaches to apply it. Thus a major effort must be pursued by both sides to understand research from a team work mentality of common objectives and participation. Taking science out of the labs is mandatory if we are looking for real application in sport sciences.

Do it right everyday

The only way to ensure long term results in any field, but especially in ours, is to continue good work with the athletes in the present and to think and plan for the future. This is obviously not an easy task and requires a great amount of creativity and applied experience by scientists working together.

The science of equilibrium

Equilibrium is always defined as the golden mean, but from our point of view the success of any sports sciences application is necessarily also related to appropriate facilities and equipment, academic support and health care. This is yet more the case when one speaks of educating developing future champions.

10
SPORT PSYCHOLOGY RESEARCH AND CONSULTING WITH ELITE ATHLETES AND COACHES

J.L. HANIN
Research Institute for Olympic Sports, Jyväskylä, Finland

Keywords: coach, Finland, IZOF, javelin throwing, mental training, psychology, research, soccer.

Introduction

It is widely recognized that contemporary elite sport can gain considerably from closer cooperation with a wide range of applied sport sciences including sociology, psychology, exercise physiology, medicine, and biomechanics. There is no doubt that all these sciences, both separately and from an interdisciplinary perspective could be especially beneficial for elite individual athletes, teams, coaches, and sports managers. However, it is also well documented that there has been always a gap between the sport scientists and practitioners (Hanin, 1989; Morgan, 1997; Sands, 1994). Moreover, anyone attempting to do applied research and consulting, especially in elite sports first has to deal with the problem of building the bridge between coaching and the task of applying scientific knowledge. Is it possible to improve collaboration between the practitioners and applied sports scientists, and if so how? What are the strengths and weaknesses of different approaches to this problem? How can one develop a model that would provide elite athletes and coaches with effective scientific 'support'? Or should it be a 'collaboration' model instead? These and other questions are critical for understanding how to enhance the performance of top athletes, coaches, managers, and media involved in elite sports. In this paper some of these questions will be addressed based on 30 years of personal experience as a researcher and consultant in the area of social and performance enhancement psychology as applied to elite sport in Russia (1967-1989) and Finland (1991-1998).

The goal of my presentation is therefore to reflect on personal and hands-on experiences in applied research and consulting in the area of sport psychology with a special reference to elite sport. I have specialized in social and sport psychology (optimal communication and performance enhancement in top sports) and became involved in both applied research and consulting in St.-Petersburg, Russia, in 1967 by combining post-graduate studies and practical work with Olympic-level Russian athletes and coaches in both individual and team sports. I was privileged to work with elite athletes and coaches both on my own and as a member of what we then called Complex (Multidisciplinary) Scientific Groups assisting athletes and coaches in the preparation for their major international competitions. Also enlightening was practical experience in psychological education of coaches working with elite athletes. Moreover, I had a chance to see how these experiences and approaches work outside Russia. Specifically, during the last 7 years, I have been working at the Research Institute for Olympic Sports (Jyväskylä, Finland) with top Finnish athletes and coaches and was able to better familiarize myself with how sport psychology is applied in several other countries of Europe and in the USA. Thus, all in all, I was privileged to work with athletes and coaches who participated in 8 Olympic games (1968 - 1998).

I will focus on my own experiences with a special reference to strengths and weaknesses of various forms of collaboration between sport psychologists (scientists) and practitioners. Suggestions will also be made for improving the working relationships between the theory and practice of sport psychology. In my paper, I will, first, briefly review key factors that are important for consideration in order to improve the quality of the cooperation between top performers and sport psychologists. I will also emphasize the individualized approach to this work and will try to demonstrate its strengths and weaknesses. In conclusion, I will try to formulate an application technology that might be used as a working model for such a cooperation. Some suggestions will be provided as to what working model is most suitable for high achievement settings such as for elite sports.

Sport Psychology Models of Cooperation in Elite Sports

Sport psychologists, like other sports scientists working with elite athletes and coaches, have implicitly or explicitly used different methods. From my personal experience, an empirical classification of at least five models can be identified: (1) the 'come and go' model, (2) the 'we have visitors' model, (3) the 'fire-brigade' model, (4) the 'team member' model, and (5) the 'let's see what can be done' model. These represent different levels of organization of collaboration between scientists and athletes/coaches and emphasis on practical issues. These approaches are briefly described in the sections that follow.

1 The 'Come and go' or 'Science first!' model

This approach is typical for a scientist whose main concern is his or her own interest in the study of some specific subject or topic that may or may not be useful or important for what athletes and coaches are doing. Thus, the focus is on generating scientific knowledge, understanding the phenomena and with minimum concern for applications. Usually, this is the first stage of any research efforts in any area of sport sciences - physiology, biomechanics, or psychology. Typically, the main product of such a study is a Masters or Ph.D. Thesis or a publication in a scientific journal with no real feedback to athletes or to a coach.

The advantages of the model: scientists (sport psychologists) better understand this particular event; a potential for the development of new and useful knowledge which might be of interest to other researchers or attract them to the problem, and a possible 'Hawthorne' (or motivational) effect in the team. The disadvantages of the model include: much delayed or no feedback to the coach and athletes; available minimum feedback might be difficult to understand and/or apply; negative impact upon athletes' and coach's attitudes to psychology and sport psychologists leads to less than effective contacts with sport scientists in future.

2 The 'We have visitors' or 'Testing again?!' model

This approach typically includes regular and routine testing 2 to 3 times a year with no individualized feedback to athletes who are usually treated as subjects. A minimum of feedback to coaches is too general and unrelated to their daily tasks and concerns. Although the data base describing different samples of athletes is growing quickly, the practical impact of such research on the training process or preparation for competition is non-existent. Again, the focus is on generating scientific knowledge that might be potentially useful for understanding the phenomena. Therefore, this model is in fact an extension of the 'Science first' model with the one exception that organizationally and financially the research is conducted on a regular basis and incurs considerable costs in time and money. Eastern European application of this model: Personality testing of all potential candidates for the national team is an example of such an approach. The advantages and disadvantages of this model are similar to the first model.

3 The 'Fire-brigade' or 'Can you help us?!' model

The approach is characterized by a different attitude from top management in elite sports. They understand the importance of sports science and expect some practical impact on the team. However, a request for help comes too late or is 'forced' on an athlete, coach or team, ignoring their willingness or readiness to cooperate, i.e. either before the competition or after a complete disaster. Additionally, it is not infrequent that political and sports leaders are too much oriented to a quick fix and expect some miracle and therefore are not interested in real collaboration between practitioners and researchers but only want to get quick results. Here is the situation when team success is the main criteria in evaluation of sports scientists' impact upon athletes and team. Some sports psychologists are also interested in serving as performance first aid since in case of success they get high visibility, media coverage and become 'top experts' overnight. However, in different countries there were many positive examples when sport psychologists were effective in serving as a fire-brigade, for instance, in Russia (Gissen, Gorbunov, Hanin, Kisselev, Rodionov, Sopov, Stambulov, Zagainov), in the USA (Balaguer, Henschen, Nideffer, Loehr, May, Murphy, Ogilvie, Ravizza, Rotella, Tutko), in Canada (Orlick), in the Czech Republic (Hosek, Vanek), to name just a few.

The advantage of this model is clearly problem- and action-oriented approach focusing on the needs of athletes, coach, and the team. Therefore the impact upon performance is anticipated and all involved are usually highly motivated. This approach is especially effective after big failures when the need for a change is clearly indicated and an outside expert serves as an agent initiating and preparing for the change and a re-examination of past efforts - both successful and less than satisfactory. A disadvantage of this model is that it is perhaps too late, followed by an overdependence on an outside expert who comes and solves our problems. Additionally, an overemphasis on practical solutions may result in not developing a scientific database from which to develop solutions. And of course an expert might fail to meet the team's high expectations.

4 'Team member' or 'That's my job!' model

The 'team member' approach is organizationally better developed than the previous forms of collaboration. Within this approach a sport psychologist is working on a regular basis as a team member with full (or part) time job responsibilities during the whole Olympic season or a cycle and is fully involved in the teams life participating in all the camps, travel, etc.. This is a practice-oriented model with no demands on research but with a major focus on the optimization of the training process, preparation for major competitions of the season, and handling sports-related and life-related problems, if any. The advantages of this model are in its being clearly problem- and action-oriented. It focuses on the needs of athletes, coach and team. A psychologist has access to important information 'from inside' and has an established status in the team and is trusted by team members and the staff. There is also no need for outside help or additional funding. However, the disadvantages or limitations of this model are related to the fact that the expert status and the skills of the team psychologist in some cases may not exactly match the tasks performed or the situations in the team. For instance the psychologist may not be qualified to solve certain problems (if she lacks a clinical background or is not well versed in the social psychological processes in the team). Furthermore, working in a team usually makes it difficult to do systematic research and therefore scientific output may be minimal. Finally, if initial psychological interventions are unsuccessful or a psychologist loses her status in the team or her relationships with key team members are broken, this may affect her future with the team. And of course, in most cases, financially it is difficult to establish a full time position for a team psychologist who would work with athletes as a staff member.

5 The 'Let's see what can be done' model

This is a most flexible form of organizing collaboration between a sport psychologist and sports team (athletes, a coach, and managerial staff). There is an established expert in sport and social or organizational psychology with good systematic contacts with elite athletes and coaches who is available for a concrete work and consulting on a regular basis. The advantages of this model are that it is a problem-oriented and situation-specific approach. A sport psychologist has a good background in research and consulting and is open and able to translate 'real problems' as verbalized by an athlete or coach into research and into consulting tasks to be solved. The focus is again on the needs of athletes, coach and team. The collaboration is based on mutual trust and professional commitments and leads to empowering both the athletes and the coach. Their joint work is also mutually enriching, both personally and professionally: athletes and coaches provide new problems and challenges for a sport psychologist who, based on past experience, helps and facilitates active experiential learning for all involved. The disadvantages of the approach include the lack of such experts, the necessity to establish preliminary contacts and working relationships, and again the expert may not be available at the time when she or he is needed.

In summary, then, all five forms of research and consulting described above reflect different organizational and intellectual resources available in a particular country. However, different emphases and a clear imbalance (concerning science or application) also reflect different stages in the development of science-practice collaboration. Recent trends indicate that in the future more and more balance should be aimed at between generating scientific knowledge and application of this knowledge in practice. Therefore, at this point, there are less and less frequent cases for the 'science first' or 'outside visitors' models, especially in elite sports. Athletes and coaches want more a problem-oriented, data-based, and situation-specific approach that can be used in their training and competitions.

On the other hand, there is growing dissatisfaction and concern about a lack of scientific basis for interventions used in elite sport (Gould & Udry, 1994; Hanin, 1997; Morgan, 1997). For instance, „most of the interventions in applied sport psychology are based upon unverified hypotheses and unsubstantiated pedagogical principles, rather than on scientific evidence" (Morgan, 1997, p.5). Therefore, one option would be to improve the quality of research in applied sport psychology and Gould and Udry (1994) suggest several 'more' directions for future research. These general recommendations include: more rigorous methodology, more focus on 'how' and 'why', more ecological validity (context), more individualized approaches, greater focus on effectiveness factors, and more effective teaching of self-regulation skills.

Another option, which is more difficult and challenging to realize, would be to try to apply the existing knowledge data base by translating it into a working model or a framework for applied research and consulting with elite athletes and coaches. Such a model is proposed and briefly described in the sections that follow.

A working model of sport psychology in elite sport

Based on my past experiences, applied sport psychology research and effective delivery of psychological services to elite athletes and coaches should be focused on two closely related aspects. These are (a) performance enhancement (high quality training, prevention of staleness and injuries, and consistent excellence in competitions), and (b) group dynamics (optimal interpersonal and intragroup communication, optimal team climate and effective management). Applied research and consulting in sport psychology could be greatly enhanced if they were based on explicitly stated guidelines. These include the following principles: action- and growth-oriented focus; more emphasis on developing individualized strengths than on correction of limitations and deficiencies; empowering athletes, coaches and teams rather than developing over-dependency on outside experts; integrating description, prediction, prevention and control; enhancing active participation, partnership, and cooperation between scientists and athletes (coaches); and finally, a holistic, multi- and interdisciplinary approach to the areas of potential growth as well as to practical problems.

Two trends have dominated in sport psychology at least during the last two decades. First, a negative and problem-oriented bias 'borrowed' from clinical psychology emphasizing correction of a person's deficiencies and limitations, by coping with stress-related emotions. Second, an overemphasis on descriptive and group-oriented comparisons of successful and less-than-successful athletes largely ignoring intra-individual dynamics. A problem with the 'group-averages' approach is that it describes mainly general trends in terms of inter-individual and inter-group differences. Therefore, by definition it is not applicable to action-oriented tasks focusing on a particular individual performing in a particular situation.

To address this problem in an elite sport setting, an idiographic (individual-oriented), empirically based approach has been developed. The Individual Zones of Optimal Functioning (IZOF) model is such a conceptual framework and assessment package that focuses on optimal and dysfunctional subjective experiences of top performers related to their successful and less-than-successful performances in practices and competitions (see Hanin, 1997 for a review). This emphasis on subjective experiences is especially relevant for skilled and expert performers. On the other hand, there is a growing awareness that ',,the most underdeveloped question in (the main stream) psychology is how people feel and experience themselves and why, when and how these self-experiences affect their action" (Sherif, 1987).

Thus, the IZOF model is proposed as a working data-based model to guide and enhance the practice of sport psychology by focusing on the individual's dynamics across different performance situations. It is outside the scope of this chapter to describe in detail the basic assumptions of the earlier version of the IZOF approach as applied to pre-competition and performance anxiety (Hanin, 1980, 1986, 1989), or its recent developments related to performance emotions and psychobiosocial states, or the assessment package using individualized mood scales (Hanin, 1992-1998).

Briefly described, the IZOF model, as illustrated by working with the Finnish Olympic-level javelin throwers (1996-1998) and soccer players (1994-1997), includes a sequence of the following action-oriented steps:

1. Listening to the coach and athlete's account of the current situation and past performance history in order to identify their concerns in training and/or in competitions that need to be addressed from the psychological point of view;
2. A brief summary of the situation and an overview of how it is handled in sport psychology in general are provided and a tentative plan of joint work on the problem at hand is proposed;
3. Data collection and processing are followed by a detailed feedback with the interpretation of results using the context-related language which is clear to the athlete and coach. As a result, an enhanced awareness and acceptance of the situation and formation of new attitudes and orientations (more constructive and positive) are acquired;
4. Based on this first discussion of preliminary findings, an action-plan for further analysis, change, and monitoring of key parameters is then jointly prepared with the aim of meeting an athlete and coach's needs in a manner fitting available resources, their life-style and current situation;
5. Checking up on the effectiveness of the program (monitoring, refining, validating initial information about practice and experiences). As a result there is developed a refined and validated program ready for further work with clear individualized criteria and markers to evaluate and assess the athlete's progress on a daily, weekly, monthly, or a season basis;
6. An individualized program developed for an athlete and coach are unique in that they aim to meet their particular needs; however, they are research-based and incorporate the principles that were already tested and validated with other top performers;
7. A sport psychologist's work in this approach is different from the traditional role of an outside expert telling others what to do or not to do. Thus, the main task is to empower an athlete and coach via an individualized approach, a predominant focus on one's strengths rather

than on deficiencies, and active participation and cooperation of all involved;

8. Feedback is provided to both coach and athlete (separately and together); therefore, their own communication and cooperation is greatly enhanced as they share new knowledge about their work and subjective emotional experiences related to their successes and failures;

9. Depending on the type of work, problem area, available resources, concrete steps and forms of follow-up during the season are planned. During the season it is also important to provide feedback and check up on how an athlete and a coach are doing;

10. Systematic contacts (phone, e-mail, fax) between an athlete, coach and a sport psychologist are also an important part of their work across the entire season. An evaluation of cooperation during the season is a good starting point for planning future work.

In summary, different steps constitute what might be called a research-consultancy cycle that includes: (a) a needs analysis, (b) focused research, (c) an immediate feedback, (d) an action plan, (e) an action, (f) an evaluation. Basically, the IZOF model is a client-oriented model that helps to structure practical work with top performers by examining a current situation based on systematic analysis of past performance history with special reference to one's successful experiences. Therefore, a problem area is always examined within the context of an individual's success-related experiences with the aim of identifying an athlete's strengths and effective coping patterns. Experiences of other top performers are also used, however, only as a tentative reference and a potential source for developing one's own strengths but never for interindividual comparisons. Self-analysis in terms of own idiosyncratic descriptors is further facilitated by a sport psychologist who helps an athlete (or coach) to be better aware and accept one's subjective experiences and to take a data-based action using this new and re-framed information. This 'three A' (Awareness, Acceptance, Action) approach proved quite effective as a guideline in the process of information gathering, processing and restructuring of the 'subjective experiences' data and planning self-regulation strategies in forthcoming tasks.

Sport Psychology Application Technology in Elite Sports

A systemic view of the elite sport environment requires, however, that a step-wise application programmes are used to enhance a research-practice-research cycle. Thus, applied and action-oriented research involving gathering preliminary information and immediate feedback followed by an action plan, joint action and evaluation is usually followed by a summary analysis and dissemination of the relevant information (via lectures, refresher courses and advanced training). This usually results in the establishment of long-term working relationships with the target (national) team of athletes and coaches who are provided with feedback and consultations during regular check-ups in the critical moments of their activity (e.g., after big successes or unexpectedly poor performances). Individualized consulting for coaches and proactive planning are the most effective strategies at this point in the collaboration between a sport psychologist and a head coach (team).

As an example, of how this approach works in practice, my recent experience of combining applied research and systematic consulting with the Finnish Olympic soccer team (U21) during the last three years are briefly described below. We started this project in 1994 with the aim of helping young players grow quickly to the international level. A series of individualized assessments involving emotion and performance profiling prior to and post- performance in all international matches was undertaken. The head coach and the players were given immediate feedback about the results of these repeated assessments. Predictions of performances based on individualized and team-level information were also conducted and combined with the individual interviews of the players. Thematic and focused motivational presentations were included into the team's routines before all international matches. This information then was summarized and presented to League soccer coaches in a module format as a part of their continuing education courses. Their feedback to this information was then used to develop the applied on-going research project extended to the U18 national team and to some local clubs. At the same time systematic consulting with the head coach was established which was wider in scope than the daily concerns of the preparation of the team.

At this point in time, the application technology looks like a four step sequence enabling action-oriented and effective response to client needs and specific situations. Thus, if a request comes from the coach or federation or sports club, first, it is immediately related to their needs, and the relevant sport-psychological research findings that might serve as a tentative database are identified. Second, the information presented in an appropriate form is then introduced to coaches (and athletes) as active participants and expert partners in joint problem solving. Then a pilot customized to the team, situation, and athletes' research and application programme is developed. As soon as a research-application cycle has been initiated, the emphasis is then shifted to the development of appropriate working skills in both coaches and athletes to enhance their potential strengths and talents. More and more work is done through distance-consulting and proactive discussion of new challenges and tasks. Therefore, athletes and coaches do not wait until some problem emerges but actively processing their current experiences to enhance learning on the job.

Mental Training and Data-based Interventions

In discussing the current situation with psychological interventions in elite sport, one important aspect is often ignored or underestimated. Specifically, training is a process of bringing a person to an agreed standard of proficiency by practice and instruction (Collins Dictionary, 1991, p.1633). Therefore, mental training aims to help a trainee become proficient in self-regulation skills enhancing performance, well-being, and mental health. Effectiveness of mental training and interventions is based on practice (it is an art!) and on understanding the underlying mechanisms (scientific basis). Historically, most mental training programmes and intervention techniques were initially based on common sense and successful practice. Now with the development of applied sport psychology, there are greater demands to provide a substantive scientific basis for mental training and interventions (Gould & Udry, 1994; Hanin, 1997; Landers, 1991, Morgan, 1997; Vealey, 1994). Better quality research is no doubt important for further development of the empirical data-base in sport psychology (Gould & Udry, 1994). However, predominantly nomothetic (group-oriented) and descriptive approaches are less than effective for individual applications. This is not to say that group-oriented research findings are useless from the applied perspective. They simply aim to answer different questions related to the sports setting at organizational and group levels. That is why, for instance, a practitioner who would like to enhance an athlete's performance by controlling her or his pre-competition anxiety in a particular situation would have a hard time using predictions or principles of the inverted-U hypothesis, or drive theory, or three-dimensional anxiety theory, or a catastrophe model, or the reversal theory.

Individualized interventions require an individually relevant empirical data-base and a completely different focus. Already mentioned IZOF model served as a framework and an assessment tool for describing, predicting, explaining, and controlling performance-related emotions in elite athletes.

It was also possible to formulate several data-base principles to guide interventions and self-regulation procedures that could be applied to a particular performer in a particular situation. Briefly described, these principles as applied to regulation of an athlete's emotions include the following seven data-based guide-lines (Hanin, 1997, 1998):

a) multi-modal principle - psychobiosocial state is conceptualized as a multi-form and multi-content entity and a target component(s) is selected for regulation;
b) multi-zone principle - specific effect (both optimal and dysfunctional) intensity is identified, refined and validated for each individual athlete;
c) multi-direction principle - current intensity is either increased or decreased in order for an athlete to enter (and exit) the optimal (dysfunctional) intensity zones;
d) multi-function principle - this helps to focus on either regulation of effort (energy production), or skill (energy utilization), or both;
e) multi-stage principle - emphasizes temporal patterns related to a preparation, task execution, and post-performance evaluation stages of activity;
f) multi-task principle - reminds about emotion patterns related to the activity structure involving several tasks performed in different contexts (practices and competitions, season-cycles);
g) multi-method principle - focuses on the necessity of using individualized and combined procedures to achieve regulation goals.

These seven data-based IZOF principles provide a concrete example of how applied research can be helpful to guide and enhance practical interventions with elite athletes and coaches. Furthermore, these interventions serve as a good basis to empirically test the validity of earlier research findings and to generate new ideas and extensions of the model thus enhancing applied research in terms of identifying new problem areas and the aspects that need to be further explored.

Future Directions in Research and Consulting

In order to enhance the effectiveness of scientific support in elite sport, several new future directions from the standpoint of research and from the practical (organizational) perspective can be identified. These include a new emphasis on the role of elite coaches in the psychological preparation of athletes and team, more focus on team-building, environmental and organizational factors, and the development of closer international cooperation between scientists, practitioners and sports organizers. Each of these aspects is briefly described in the sections that follow.

More Psychological Support for Elite Coaches

The initial focus of most sport psychology research and interventions with athletes and partly with teams is well documented in literature from various countries. It is my contention, however, that the role of elite coaches in the psychological preparation of athletes and teams should be further re-emphasized. In practice, it means that an elite coach should be a central figure in preparation of the team and sport psychologists should work more through the coach and with the coach-athlete team rather than only with an athlete. Additionally, enhancing the psychological competence of elite coaches could be a decisive factor in the future.

In the past, sport-psychological interventions and mental training programmes were usually focused mainly on competing athletes (coping with competition stressors). Less attention was paid to high quality practices and prevention of overtraining, staleness, burn-out, and injuries. I believe that the most urgent and promising area of research and applications in sport psychology in the future will be the optimal performance of elite coaches and their coping skills of handling both short-term (Zagaloí effect) and long term chronic (burn-out) stresses. Special qualitative research into careers of outstanding coaches and identifying the factors of their consistent excellence would be a challenge for future researchers and practitioners. On the applied side, it would be important to summarize existing experiences of how continuing individualized consulting can be better arranged for elite coaches to help them anticipate critical transition periods or 'passages' (G. Sheer) in their careers.

Team-building and Effective Management

Traditionally, social psychological research in sport psychology comprises 8-10% of all efforts and the role of environmental, organizational factors in elite sport is still underestimated (Hanin, 1993). Sport psychology should therefore focus more on holistic approach to the interpersonal and group processes that are determining the performance and life of a team in a wider social and cross-cultural context. Optimization of communication in the team is a very promising and productive area of research and application (Hanin, 1992). At the practical level, team building with elite athletes has been initiated in the late 1960's with top Russian female volleyball teams and was used as a system with the Russian Rowing Team before the Montreal Olympics in 1976. A similar approach was used by Gloria Balaguer and Jerry May with the US track and field team before and during the Barcelona Olympics and by Christine LeScanff with the French Sailing Team. However, in all these cases a sport psychologist usually works directly with athletes. Recently, in my work with the Finnish National track and field team before and during European Championships in Budapest (1998), we tried out a completely different approach (distance-consulting with the head coach and team leaders) that worked exceptionally well and seems promising for the future.

Practically nothing is known about the psychology of effective management in elite teams, sports federations, and clubs. Considering the rapid development of elite sports, areas such as organizational development, change, and change management potentially could be very important new directions for research and applications. No doubt, the experiences and practices of organizational psychology and management already available in settings other than high achievement sport could be beneficial for elite sports. On the other hand, applied research findings in elite sports might be of certain interest to management, army, police, etc.

Cross-cultural adaptation of athletes and coaches

Recent developments in European elite sports indicate that more elite athletes and coaches will be working abroad. Therefore, new skills and cross-cultural competence will be necessary in order to adapt to new conditions and environmental demands, to say nothing about quick adjustments in a new team, finding a common language between new team-mates and a coach. A preliminary experience of general and specific cross-cultural preparation of Olympic level soccer players (half of the U21 team already works abroad) indicate that developing an orientation and skills to cope with the media, quick adaptation in the target team, and the basics of negotiation skills could be especially useful. This work is expected to continue by getting first-hand feed-back from these players' entry in leading European soccer teams. Another sample that is worthy of special study is NHL players from different countries.

With more migration and higher mobility rates among elite coaches, a critical factor is the assessment of a candidate's potential for cross-cultural adaptation and individualized programmes aimed at facilitating his or her entry into a host country. This is especially important in view of the fact that tradition and values in different European countries are different and the well meaning but authoritarian coach with a clear orientation on success can be less than effective starting his work in an amateurish environment of the host country. A follow up with the coach or athlete could be also instrumental in helping them to quickly adapt and function effectively both professionally and personally in the new environment.

International cooperation between scientists, practitioners and sports organizers.

There is a trend indicating that in the future improved collaboration between sports scientists, practitioners and sports organizers (politicians) from different European countries is needed. Therefore, an International Sports Science Coordination Centre may help identify what is known and works best in the field (available products) and to prioritize the areas that warrant further collaborative both for research and applications in the future. An example of such efforts in the area of sport psychology is the first Nordic Meeting (in Stockholm, May 26-27, 1998) that has addressed the issue of how to improve cooperation between the Danish, Finnish Norwegian, and Swedish, sport psychologists working with elite athletes and coaches.

National and international bodies can stimulate improved cooperation between European sport scientists, for instance, through joint funding of high-priority applied interdisciplinary research, application, and coaches' training programs. However, in several European countries with good resources in top athletes and coaches (for instance, in Austria), there is a lack of experts in the area of sport psychology who could provide high quality services (in research and application) for elite athletes and coaches. One possible solution would be to use the expertise of internationally recognized applied researchers and practitioners in sport psychology who could deliver the necessary services for elite athletes, teams and coaches and provide hands-on experience for local young aspiring sport psychologists interested in working with elite performers.

Conclusion

I already had the opportunity to suggest some ways to improve research and application in sport psychology (Hanin, 1979, 1980, 1989). Now as never before, a delivery system for applying what is already available in sport psychology and other sub-disciplines is important. The things I mentioned briefly in this presentation are important for each sport science discipline, as is apparent. At the same time it is important to stress that the best results both in research and application can be achieved if athletes and coaches are offered inter and multidisciplinary knowledge that helps them better see the meaning of their work in a more holistic way without too much compartmentalization, as has been the case in the past.

Several factors are important to consider before a model of collaboration between sports scientists and practitioners can be proposed. First, top performers are usually highly motivated people who have developed their own approach to performance and actively use their own experience to enhance consistent excellence. Therefore, applied research in this setting should be client-centered, action-oriented and should fit well into the environment. On the other hand, applications should be focused on the dynamics of their own individual performance, better self-awareness and self-acceptance, and effective self-regulation. Such a self-referenced and mastery-oriented approach is most productive from both the personal and professional growth perspectives, as well as for long-term mental health. As a result, athletes and coaches learn to turn a 'bad' day into successful performance in sport and life and achieve consistent excellence.

References

Gould, D., Tammen, V., Murphy, S., & May, J. (1989). An examination of U.S. Olympic sport psychology consultants and services they provide. The Sport Psychologist, 3, 300-312.

Hanin Y. L. & Martens, R. (1978). Sport Psychology in the USSR. Coaching Review, 1 (3), 38-41.

Hanin, Y. L. (1980) Applying sport psychology: past, present, and future. In: C.H. Nadeau (ed.) Psychology of Motor behavior and Sport, Proceedings of the NASPPA 1979 Annual Conference, (pp. 37-48). Champaign: Human Kinetics.

Hanin, Y. L. (1989) Applying Sport Psychology: International and Cross-Cultural Perspectives. Proceedings of the First IOC World Congress on Sport Sciences (pp. 359-363). Colorado Springs: USOC.

Hanin, Y. L. (1992) Social Psychology and Sport : Communication Processes in Top Performance Teams. Sports Science Review , 1 (2), pp. 13-28.

Hanin, Y. L. (1993) Organizational Psychology in Sport Setting. Revista de Psicologia del Deporte. No. 3 , pp. 17-30.

Hanin. Y. L. (1997, August). Mental Training: Does It Work? A keynote address at the 2nd Annual Congress of the European College of Sport Sciences (ECSS). Copenhagen, Denmark.

Morgan, W. P. (1997). Mind Games: The Psychology of Sport. In: D R Lamb & R. Murray (Eds.). Perspective in Exercise Science and sport Medicine, (Vol. 10, Optimizing Sport Performance). (pp. 1-62). Carmel, In: Cooper Publishing Company.

Sands, W. P. (1994). How can coaches use sport science? Track Coach, pp. 4280-4283, 4292.

Vealey, R. S. (1994). Current status and prominent issues in sport psychology interventions. Medicine and Science in Sports and Exercise, 26, 495 - 502.

11
PERSONALITY, PERFORMANCE AND ROLE CONFLICTS IN ELITE SPORT

G. BREIVIK
Norwegian University of Sport and Physical Education

Keywords: MAPE-test, Norway, performance, personality, profile, role conflict, sensation seeking, social network, test.

Introduction

Modern elite sport is increasingly based on scientific research. The Norwegian University for Sport and Physical Education (NUSPE) has played a central role in sport research in Norway after the institution was established in 1968. In Norway all sport, both mass and elite sport, is organized in one sport organization, the Norwegian Sport Federation (NIF). Since the late 1980s collaboration in sport research between NUSPE and NIF has been increasing. The Norwegian Sport Federation has established an Elite Sport Center and an Olympic Sport Program (Olympiatoppen) with around 150 athletes who are sponsored by the Ministry of Cultural Affairs and the Norwegian Sport Federation. The Elite Sport center is adjacent to the sport university (NUSPE) with proximity for strong links in research and sport development.

The successful Norwegian Olympic Program has had the following objectives:

A) Think holistically or systemically, with the athlete in the center. Think about success in sport but also about health, social network and welfare.
B) Cross-fertilize between disciplines. Learn from other sports and from successful coaches and athletes.
C) Utilization of highly qualified coaches, educated at NUSPE, has been instrumental for success in several sports such as soccer, Nordic and alpine skiing, ski-jumping, track athletics.
D) Basic training at the Elite Sport Center is built on scientific principles and research. However in a recent research report Olympic athletes were least satisfied with collaboration with scientists and most satisfied with coaches and the training facilities. There is much to improve in the

collaboration between science and sport.

Personally I think that we have three easy targets for improvement:

1) We need to scan and harvest international research in a more systematic way to build strong knowledge and competence bases over time.
2) We need more research that originates in the sport system itself.
3) We need to plough information and knowledge from science back into the sport system in a much more consistent and efficient way. I have myself been very happy in my work with the Elite Sport Center and the Olympic athletes. In the following I provide four examples of how this collaboration has worked.

Personality and Sensation Seeking in Elite Sport

Since 1983 I have been engaged in research on elite sport athletes from a psychological perspective in which we have looked at similarities and differences between types of sports. I will give you a glimpse of that research in the following. The main variables in this research have been related to personality, both general and specific traits, like sensation seeking, anxiety, achievement motivation, risk taking and others (see Breivik, 1996a; 1996b). We also studied athletes in specific situations where psychological states and behavioral reactions were observed. In the following I will present some results related to one specific variable called «sensation seeking». «Sensation seeking» is «a trait defined by the need for varied, novel, and complex sensations and experiences and the willingness to take physical and social risks for the sake of such experience» (Zuckerman 1979:10). There are four subfactors that comprise the total sensation seeking trait. The subfactors of the Sensation Seeking Scale are summarized by Zuckerman (1983:286) in the following way:

1. The Thrill and Adventure Seeking Scale (TAS) contains items indicating a desire to engage in risky and adventurous activities and sports (skydiving, climbing, scuba diving, skiing, sailing).
2. The Experience Seeking Scale (ES) contains items representing the seeking of stimulation through the mind and the senses, through music, art, travel, psychedelic drugs and meeting unusual or unconventional people.
3. The Disinhibition Scale (Dis) contains items representing sensation

seeking through drinking, partying, gambling and sexual variety.
4. The Boredom Susceptibility Scale (BS) contains items representing an aversion to repetition whether in work or with people, and restlessness and boredom when such constancy is unavoidable.

The results of our studies showed that athletes in high, medium and low risk sports had different personality profiles. There was an almost linear association between level of risk and sensation seeking profile (Fig. 1). This was true in both individual and team sports.

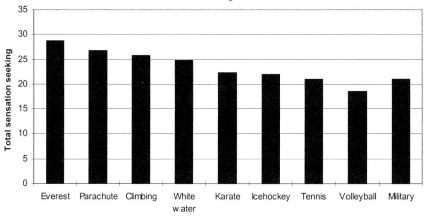

Fig. 1. Total sensation seeking scores of elite male athletes in different sports, compared with a control group of military recruits.

In individual sports we compared high risk climbers with medium risk karate athletes and low risk tennis players. All athletes were male, on national teams, and among the very best in their sport. We used Zuckerman's Sensation Seeking Scale, Form V in Norwegian translation to test sensation seeking. Table 1 presents the results with t-tests between the different groups.

Table 1. Sensation seeking scores (scale V), means and standard deviations, among Norwegian elite climbers, n=18, national team karate athletes, n=17, and national team tennis players, n=5.

	TAS		ES		DIS		BS		TOTAL	
	Mean	St.d.	Mean	St.d.	Mean	St.d.	Mean	St.d.	Mean	St.d.
Climber	8.7	1.2	7.6	1.8	6.5	2.5	4.4	2.1	27.2	5.1
Karate	8.0	2.3	4.8	2.2	5.7	2.3	3.8	2.2	22.3	6.4
Tennis	7.6	1.8	5.2	1.6	6.4	1.2	1.8	0.4	21.0	2.0

Statistical significance: *p<0.05, **p<0.005, ***p<0.001

	TAS	ES	DIS	BS	TOTAL
Climb./karate	ns	***	ns	ns	*
Climb./tennis	ns	*	ns	*	*
Tennis/karate	ns	ns	ns	ns	ns

The climbers score higher than the other groups, especially on ES and Total but also with a clear tendency on TAS and BS. In a similar way we found in team sports that skydivers scored higher than ice hockey players and volleyball players.

Table 2. Sensation seeking scores (scale V), means and standard deviations, among Norwegian national team skydivers, n=20, ice hockey players, n=18, and volleyball players, n=13.

	TAS		ES		DIS		BS		TOTAL	
	Mean	St.d.	Mean	St.d.	Mean	St.d.	Mean	St.d.	Mean	St.d.
Skydive	8.8	1.0	6.9	2.3	6.5	2.6	4.6	2.0	26.7	5.5
Icehockey	7.2	2.1	4.5	1.4	5.7	1.8	4.4	2.2	21.7	4.2
Volleyball	5.2	2.4	4.0	2.1	4.9	2.7	4.4	1.7	18.5	5.0

Statistical significance: *p<0.05, **p<0.005, ***p<0.001

	TAS	ES	DIS	BS	TOTAL
Skydive/icehock.	**	**	ns	ns	**
Skydive/volley	***	**	ns	ns	***
Icehock./volley	*	ns	ns	ns	(0.07)

This information is useful both in relation to sports counseling, selection procedures and adjustment inside a given sport. The results were always discussed individually and also, if necessary, collectively with the teams. Sometimes we discovered maladjusted athletes, like a high sensation seeking tennis player with a lot of talent, but psychologically in the wrong sport. We also found relevant differences inside a given sport. When we tested the Alpine skiing team before the season with the successful international breakthrough ten years ago, we found that all the downhill skiers had higher sensation seeking scores and different profiles from the typical slalom skiers. It takes a special psychological makeup to love the high speed, the fast reactions, the thrills, but also the fears of a downhill ski slope. In volleyball we found that the most aggressive smashers were high sensation seekers and the players lowest in sensation seeking were defensive players. The same was true in one of our best teams in soccer, where the goal-scoring forwards had highest sensation seeking scores followed by the defensive players while the middle field players were lowest.

Not only on the field, or in the arena, are the differences relevant. Coaches need to relate to athletes during training camps and competitions. High sensation seekers do not tolerate boredom, they are impulsive and social, needing variation. Various studies have shown that they are more likely to break rules, drive too fast, drink too much, seek out situations with thrills, try gambling, go to parties, test forbidden drugs, improvise dangerous stunts (Zuckerman, 1994). Elite athletes are normally disciplined and well educated people. Nevertheless there are differences in personality that are useful to take into consideration for coaches and leaders, and also for the athletes themselves.

Coping with high stress situations. Some studies of skydiving.

The purpose of the following four studies was to get a better theoretical, methodological, and empirical basis for understanding why, and how, different people react, cope and perform during highly stressful situations, like skydiving. Classical studies, like Fenz & Epstein (1967), and Ursin, Baade & Levine (1978), did not take systematic account of differences in personality. They did not study activation(heart rate) during the jump and they did not relate personality to differences in excitation, psychological states (anxiety) and performance.

Study 1. The Personality of Skydivers
Is there a specific skydiver personality, or are people who jump "ordinary people"? Different aspects of the problem are discernible:

1) All those who want to try skydiving may be quite different from other people.
2) Those who drop out after a few jumps may be different from those that

continue with jumping.

3) Among those who continue, those who jump a lot and become experts, may be different from the rest. A filter model was developed to test our hypotheses (see Fig. 2). The filters are supposed to be personality-related variables, some of them are hypothesized in the model.

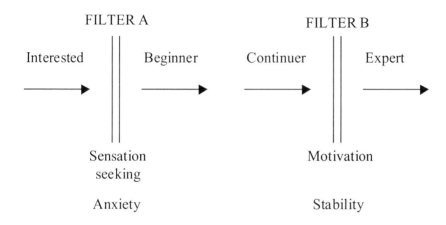

Fig. 2. A filter model of the selection process in skydiving

In the first study we used a battery of well known personality tests: MMPI, Cattell 16 PF, Zuckerman Sensation Seeking Scale V. All were in Norwegian translation and with acceptable reliability scores. The following samples were tested: 20 elite national team jumpers, 27 experienced jumpers (average 700 jumps), 32 drop outs (less than 10 jumps). The control groups were 43 sport students and 28 ordinary military recruits.

The results showed that the biggest difference in scores was between the parachute groups on one hand and the control groups (sport students and military recruits) on the other. All skydivers seemed to have a "strong nervous system" (Pavlov), a strong activity in the septal-lateral approach system (high impulsivity), and dominant parasympathetic autonomic reactions (low anxiety). The high performance groups had higher scores on psychopathy (Pd+), extraversion (Si-), boldness (H+), and imagination (M+), compared with drop outs.

The results showed that the big question is whether to jump or not to jump. When you have jumped, other factors (time, money, travel distance) seem to decide whether you continue. Among jumpers those who jump a lot seem to have more extreme profiles than the rest, especially on extraversion and psychopathy.

Study 2.   Skydivers compared with other risk sport athletes

Is there a common personality profile across different risk sports? The aspect of serious risk, the opportunity for strong sensations, and the possibility of unusual experiences, are common to climbing, skydiving, and white water kayaking. But there are also specific aspects of each activity in relation to both environment, bodily movement and psychological demands.

The risk sport groups consisted of top level athletes: 38 elite climbers, 31 white water kayakers, 20 skydivers. The control groups consisted of 26 military recruits and 43 sport students. The groups were tested with a general personality test, Cattell 16 PF and Zuckerman's Sensation Seeking Scale V (SSS V). All groups were male.

The results showed that the high risk athletes scored high on drive factors like dominance (E+), imagination (M+) and independence (IV+) on Cattell 16PF. They also had high needs in relation to Thrill and adventure seeking (TAS), and New experiences (ES), on the sensation seeking scale. They had lower avoidance, or "stop factors", with weak super-ego (G-) and low ergic tension (Q4-) on Cattell 16 PF.

The different risk sport groups had specific profiles. The skydivers were more outgoing and extroverted and had lower anxiety. The climbers tended to be more aggressive, imaginative and independent. The kayakers were more reserved and cool than the other groups. All three sport groups had higher scores on intelligence and were more liberal than sport students and military recruits. The high risk athletes had been involved in significantly more other high risk sports than the controls, and were more willing to take risks.

To sum up there seems to be some common personality characteristics of high risk athletes across differences in specific sports. At the same time there are differences that may be caused by the uniqueness of each sport or by more accidental subcultural influences. Research across cultural differences and over time will answer this question.

In another study of elite skydivers and climbers a few years later we found a similar pattern. Both climbers and skydivers had strong drive factors and had high scores on risk taking.   But the skydivers seemed to be more team-players. They were more extroverted, impulsive and had low anxiety. The climbers were more introverted and individualistic, with strong aggressiveness and independence. This was also found in a study of Everest climbers (Breivik, 1996).

Study 3.   The prediction of drop out and success

If skydivers have a specific personality profile it should be possible to develop a test that predicts drop out and success. Several accidents in skydiving seem to be caused by an overload of stress and a failure to perform emergency procedures. There may be a "right stuff" personality in parachuting and also a "wrong stuff". These categories may be discrete or continuous.

On the basis of the first study a test was developed that contained the best predictive scales from MMPI, Cattell 16PF and SSS V. The test was called MAPE and included Extraversion, Psychopathy, Ego strength, Imagination and Affectothymia. 508 skydivers were tested before their first jump. Their jump record was then tracked continuously during the following two years. A sample of 162 experienced jumpers and a sample of 179 military recruits were used as respectively a comparison and a control group (Johnsen, 1996).

The results showed that there was a significant difference on the MAPE -scale between skydivers and controls. There was no significant difference on the MAPE scale between continuers (n=429) and drop outs (n=79). Those who jumped a lot and became good, "the right stuff", scored significantly higher on the MAPE scale. There was an almost linear relationship between MAPE- score on one hand, and performance level and certification level on the other hand (Fig. 3).

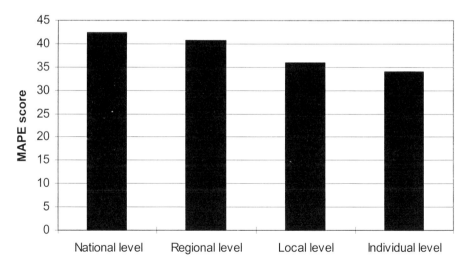

Fig. 3. The MAPE score of skydivers at various competition levels, from single individuals jumping for fun (n=52), to jumpers at local (n=122), regional (n=31) and national (n=28) competition levels.

The MAPE -test did not do the job it was designed for. It could not pick out the continuers from the drop outs. It was however able to predict very well the level of performance among the experienced jumpers. Maybe it is easier to predict the "right stuff" than the "wrong stuff". It seems to be even more difficult to pick out what we called "the dangerous stuff", those who continue to jump but for the wrong reasons, and who typically end up dead with an unopened reserve parachute on their back.

Study 4. Personality and activation in novice and expert skydivers

How is personality related to psychological states and to physiological activation while jumping? We wanted to make a replica of Fenz & Epstein's (1967) classical study with better procedures and measuring devices (Roth, Breivik, Jørgensen & Hofman, 1996).

Fenz and Epstein found that experienced skydivers had a peak in subjective fear and heart rate before the jump whereas the inexperienced had a peak when they exited from the plane. Fear and heart rate levels were lower among experienced jumpers. The experienced jumpers seemed to have learned to inhibit and control their fear. Fenz and Epstein did not systematically study personality differences, but found that novices who performed well had similar physiological reactions (heart rate, respiration rate and skin conductance) as experienced jumpers. Experienced jumpers who performed badly were similar to novices in their reactions.

Ambulatory heart and respiration rates were measured (with the Koelner Vitaport System) in 16 novice and 25 expert sport skydivers (>380 delayed free-fall jumps) while making a static-line jump. Psychological state tests were taken on the ground before the jump, while sitting in the plane just before the jump, and after the jump. Trait tests included Eysenck's Personality Questionnaire, Zuckerman's Sensation Seeking Scale V and Spielberger's STAI Trait/State.

The results showed that self-reported anxiety and heart rate peaked near the point of jumping in both groups, rather than earlier in experts, as reported by Fenz & Epstein (1967). While sitting in the airplane 1 min. before exit, mean heart rate was 124 bpm in novices and 102 in experts, and increased during jumping to 170 and 145 respectively.

Also respiration rate and self-rated anxiety made after the jump showed curves similar to the heart rate curves, with a peak for both groups at exit from the plane.

Experts scored higher than novices on Psychoticism and Experience seeking. Those who scored high on Thrill and Adventure Seeking had low state anxiety scores. The jumpers with high Psychoticism scores had a lower increase in heart rate before the jump. Among experienced jumpers persons with high Extraversion scores showed lower heart rates at exit. A regression analysis showed that among experienced jumpers the best predictor of heart rate at exit from plane was the number of jumps the skydivers had made.

Fenz and Epstein's results were not replicated. There is no sign of inhibition of fear but rather of a gradual decrease in activation and fear with increased experience. Personality variables do not seem to have a decisive influence on excitation, with the exception of extraversion and psychoticism. Experience is more important than personality at this level. But as we saw, personality is important for the decision whether to jump or not.

In a study of 10 Norwegian national team ski jumpers who were tested in a recent study, while making their first parachute jumps, we found that those who performed best were extroverts and high sensation seekers who had few defense mechanisms, but to our surprise high heart rates. The jumper who had the lowest heart rate performed poorly and scored very high on defense mechanisms. People high in defense mechanisms seem to use their mental processing capacity on non-relevant tasks. It seems to be much more efficient to use few defense mechanisms, let activation get high and stay focused on the task.

Conclusions

The theories of Eysenck and Zuckerman seem to account well for some general aspects of skydiving, but not for the details. Skydivers have strong drive factors (extraversion, psychoticism, sensation seeking), and low avoidance factors (neuroticism, anxiety, defense mechanisms, super-ego). The jumpers who jump a lot and become good, have more extreme personality profiles. Several personality traits seem to be linked to performance, but there is no easy discernible relationship with psychological states and physiological activation. Whereas earlier theories looked for low activation, it seems that strong activation may be linked to good performance, even in beginners. Further studies should test both the catastrophe theory of increasing breakdown of performance in highly anxious subjects (high in defense mechanisms), and a possibility of a more linear relationship in performance and activation in low anxiety subjects.

It should also be mentioned that in our studies of skydivers, and especially in the study of the national team in ski-jumping, we always discussed our results with both the skydivers and the coach. This was done both in individual sessions and collectively. We found that we were often able to confirm intuitions of the coach and the athletes, and also express and explain our findings in ways that made sense. In this way the feedback could be used in new training sessions and helped to provide a basis for further improvement.

Tensions and paradoxes in the role model of top level athletes

Introduction
In the media the lives of top level athletes are portrayed in very different ways. Sometimes the focus is on the harsh and tough training, the monotonous life, the forsaken pleasures. Other times the focus is on the privileges, the travels, the support system, the glories. And then again emphasis is put on the pressure, the expectations from the public, the short way from the pinnacle to the bench. And recently the media are more and more filled with stories of huge signing sums, bonuses and profits, and of the millionaire life. The situation is very different from sport to sport, from country to country, but certainly the role model of top level athletes in general has changed significantly in one generation, from the moderate training, the amateur and hobby character, the play element, in the beginning of the 1970s to the professionalized athletes of the 1990s with a lot of training, hard work, strong media focus, possible damage to health, and the involvement of big money. It seems that in many ways the transition has gone too fast. If this is so we would expect interesting tensions and paradoxes in the top level athlete role model. In a recent study of Norwegian Olympic athletes we tried to find out how the present situation for top level athletes is in regard to standard of living, quality of life, and role model expectations.

Methods
88 top level athletes, 44 women and 48 men, from 27 different sports, answered a questionnaire with questions about social background, athletic conditions, social network, income and work, economics, education, life style, and quality of life. The athletes were all members of the Olympic Top Team sponsored by the State and Olympic Committee, which at that time comprised 135 athletes altogether. The average age for male athletes was 28.5 years, for women 26.5. The athletes represented summer and winter sports, team and individual sports and came from small and big sports, and from poor and rich sport federations.

In the following we will report findings in relation to three problem areas:
1) Economics and work,
2) health and injuries, and

3) quality of life and happiness.

Results

1) 50% of the athletes considered sport to be work, 41% looked at sport as a hobby and the rest thought "both work and hobby". This means that the professionalization and work attitude has not become totally dominant, even if the athlete has an average of 17.5 hours effective training and used 8.2 hours in average for transportation. In addition comes the preparation, the work on equipment, planning etc., which should leave little time for ordinary work.

   50% of the athletes have no ordinary work, whereas 26% work full time and the rest part time. This means that some athletes have a week where work and sport take 10 hours per day. It is therefore not surprising that more than 30% think that work is the biggest obstacle to sufficient and satisfactory training conditions. However their are different strategies. Around 30% of the athletes who do not work earn less than 100 000 kroner which is far below average in the population and far below the athletes that work. They choose to stay poor and train. The other biggest non-working group is those who earn more than 800 000 Norwegian kroner, the sport millionaires, who comprise 12.2% of the non-working athletes. That means that by dropping work and going full-time professionally you may become very poor or very rich, depending on the sport, the sponsor, the media focus and so on.

2) What about the health situation? On average the athletes had 28.2 days last year when they were unable to train normally due to injuries. The longest break in training during their career amounted to an average of 71 days. On a scale with three alternatives "little", "medium", and "often/ a lot", only half of the athletes say they have little pain. 13% of the athletes have a lot of pain. It is therefore not surprising that only 57% of the athletes feel sure that top level sport is positive for their health. 36% in fact feel that to a varying degree they damage their bodies by being top level athletes.

   In spite of this situation, when asked how important various factors in life are for happiness and life fulfillment, the number one factor for the athletes, as for the population in general, is health. 83 percent of the athletes thought that «good health» was very important. So why then do they engage in an activity for 10-15 years of their life that, for a lot of them, is harmful and painful?

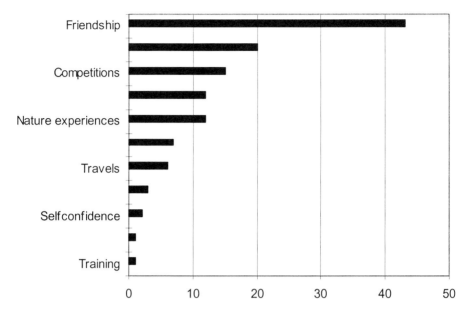

Fig. 4. «What is the most important joy/positive factor in your sport practice?». Number
of answers given to various factors. Some athletes have given more than one
factor. Categories established post hoc. (Number of athletes = 87)

3) When asked about what is the most positive factor, the most important
joy, in sport, 51% of the athletes said "achievement, success". This is
not very surprising when one has put several years of ones life into hard
training to become number one, to have success. However when asked
about what is important in life to achieve happiness, the athletes ranked
"success in sport" as number 16 out of 17. Only 17% of the top level
athletes thought success in sport was very important to make them happy.
Health, stable family life, close friends, love and respect were the most
important factors (Fig. 5). Also the importance of regular physical training
was ranked low, in fact lower than in the general population of the same
age. 37.5% thought regular physical training was very important. How
is it possible on one hand that success is the biggest joy in sport, and on
the other success in sport is not very important to become happy in life?

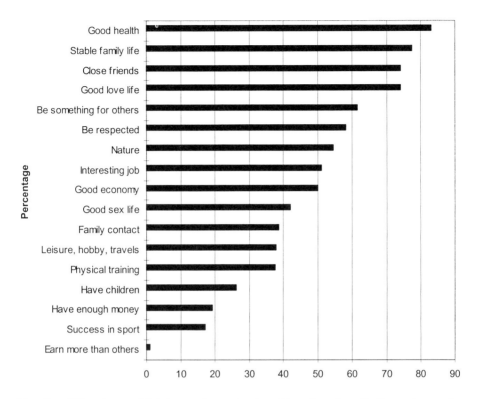

Fig. 5. «What do you think is very important to achieve happiness?» Percentages who have answered «very important» to the various factors. (N=87)

Discussion

The top level athletes live in a tension between the amateur and the professional role model. Some sports are more professionalized than others, but many top level athletes have a choice between full time training and poverty on one hand, and work and a good economic standard, but with less satisfactory training conditions, on the other. Only relatively few athletes in Norway are fully professional and rich athletes. As training loads increase and new levels of performance have to be met, athletes will have to adopt a fully professionalized role model. Probably very little will be left over from the amateur ideas and role models.

The heavy training and tough competition lead to injuries, pain and health problems. At the same time health is seen as the most important factor for happiness in life. The athletes seem to handle this by adopting a schizophrenic view: Sport is not a part of my normal life, it is a long «time out» with its own logic and rules. This reasoning also seems to explain why success is the most important factor for joy in sport but not important for happiness in ones life. Sport is a special sector, or a period in life, which has not much to do with ordinary life. However this may be an illusion. A top level athletic career does not lead to a "normal life" afterwards, but to a life that in many ways, is imprinted by the sports career.

It may soon become like it is in ballet where the dancers retire when they are around 40 years old, without having to start a new work career. In a similar way the athletes in the future will probably have one single identity, one role model in life, that of being a top level athlete.

Why did the best become best?

Our present study, which has just been finished, examines the life and development of the 18 best athletes in Norway today to learn more about how they grew up and how they developed into being the best. We picked those with the best results from Olympic Games, World Championships and World Cups during the last 4 years, and compared them with a matched group of athletes who did not succeed in the same manner. All athletes came from individual sports. The following hypotheses were developed in collaboration with the leaders of the Elite Sport Center: The best athletes a) play much b) specialize early c) train hard from early age d) vary training and e) have strong support from father (and mother). The preliminary results show that hypothesis a, d and e were supported, whereas b was refuted, and c partly confirmed. The best athletes played a lot, were very active in organized and unorganized contexts, specialized later, and continued longer with other sports in addition to the one they became the best in. They were more inner directed, enjoyed hard training and had very strong support from the family. They did not have very clear idols, were not determined at early age to become a world class athlete. The success came gradually and was caused by hard training and will combined with talent. They felt that those who become the very best in the world have certain psychological skills, a strong will and a «killer instinct». Most of them felt that the children who grow up today do not have the opportunities for vigorous play and strong exercise as they themselves had. Modern life is too soft and too much an indoor life. That will influence the quality of elite sport in the future.

These are just a few of the results from the study. It poses interesting questions and challenges for those who want to prepare and lay the groundwork for future world-class athletes.

Conclusion

I have tried to present some of the theories, methods and results of studies that I have conducted on elite sport athletes in collaboration with the Elite Sport Center and the Norwegian Sport Federation. I have enjoyed this work tremendously. As I said, the athletes themselves feel that they need better cooperation with scientists. Certainly elite sport in the future, to put it paradoxically, will be an advanced form of art, built on scientific research. We should look forward to take part in this endeavor.

References

1. Breivik, B. (1995a) Personality, sensation seeking and arousal in high risk sports. NUSPE. Oslo.
2. Breivik, G. (1995b) Empirical studies of sensation seeking in sports. NUSPE. Oslo.
3. Breivik, G. (1996) «Personality, Sensation Seeking and Risk Taking among Everest Climbers.» International Journal of Sport Psychology. Vol. 27, No. 3, pp. 308-320
4. Eysenck, H.J. & Eysenck, M.W. (1985). Personality and individual differences. A natural science approach. New York and London: Plenum Press.
5. Fenz, W.D. & Epstein, S. (1967). Gradients of physiological arousal in skydivers. Psychosomatic Medicine, 29, 33-51
6. Gilberg, R., Breivik, G. (1997): Gjennom slit til stjernene (Per ardua ad astra). NIH. Oslo.
7. Hardy, L. & Parfitt, G. (1991) A catastrophe model of anxiety and performance. British Journal of Psychology, 82, 163-178
8. Johnsen, J.H. (1994) Personality and Prediction. Retention, Success and Accident Proneness. NUSPE. Oslo.
9. Roth, W.T., Breivik, G., Jørgensen, P.E and Hofman, J. (1996) Activation in novice and expert skydivers while jumping. Psychophysiology, 33, 63-77
10. Zuckerman, M. (1979) *Sensation Seeking. Beyond the Optimal Level of Arousal.* . Hillsdale, New Jersey: Lawrence Erlbaum Associates.
11. Zuckerman, M. (1983) Sensation Seeking and Sports. *Personality and Individual Differences*, Vol. 4, No. 3, pp. 285-293
12. Zuckerman, M. (1985) *Preliminary Manual for Form VI of the Sensation Seeking Scale (SSS VI)*. Newark: University of Delaware.
13. Zuckerman, M. (1994) Behavioral expressions and biosocial bases of

sensation seeking. Cambridge: Cambridge University Press.

14. Vikne, J.: Hva karakteriserer toppidrettsutøveren? En studie av bakgrunnen til idrettsutøverne tilknyttet Olympiatoppen 1994. NIH. Oslo. 1996

15. Ursin, H., Baade, E. & Levine, S. (eds.). (1978). Psychobiology of stress: A study of coping men. New York: Academic Press.

12
PHYSIOTHERAPY IN SPORTS: THEORETICAL BACKGROUNDS AND PRACTICAL CONSEQUENCES

J. CABRI and J. GOMES-PEREIRA
Faculdade de Motricidade Humana, Universidade Técnica de Lisboa, Lisbon, Portugal

Keywords: education program, isokinetics, physiotherapy, Portugal, sport physio-therapist, sport specific movement.

Introduction

In physiotherapy many specialties exist, each delineating a specific area of interest. One of the most popular areas of specialization in Europe is represented through the sports physical therapy interest groups. Indeed, of the sixteen member organizations of the Standing Liaison Committee of Physiotherapists of the European Union, fourteen countries reported having one or another activity specifically interested in sports physical therapy (SLCP, 1998).

The sports physical therapist (also sport physiotherapist - SPT) is a professional who is involved in the rehabilitation of injured athletes and in the prevention of sports injuries. Presenting solutions to performance related problems due to physiological, biomechanical, pathological, and/or psychological factors are thought also to be within the competency of the SPT. The SPT is also known to be active on the field, during competition or training sessions, in order to provide either first aid after injury or to consult the trainer/coach on the playing capabilities of individuals. Furthermore, SPT's are also extending their activities in providing assistance for athletes and their environment (relatives, parents, organizations, federations).

However, some redundant factors still exist preventing the SPT to be a recognized member of the team of health care providers in a sport or exercise context. These factors are based on different grounds such as gaps in education, competency conflicts, economic priorities, training and performance objectives, but are rarely based on assessments of efficacy in intervention. This may be due to a lack of availability of good scientific data.

Although many post-basic courses (or post-graduate courses) in sports physical therapy are organized in the various European countries, there is a great diversity with respect to their aims and objectives, contents and contact hours (i.e. real hours of teaching versus accumulated hours from other specialties). This provides in the profession of physical therapy one of the most popular specialties in post-basic education, although its range of competency is still under much discussion.

The relationship between athlete, coach, and members of the medical team is of utmost importance for establishing efficient rehabilitation programs. However, that the place of the SPT is somewhat dubious for both performance-related and medical issues may put pressure on the rehabilitation program. Moreover, economic issues may create some incompatibilities between the condition of the patient and his/her capabilities to perform at a high level, according to the physiological and psychological re-adaptation processes. Therefore, education in sports physical therapy should focus not only on sports-medical and sports science related topics, but also on psychological issues, such as stress management, fear avoidance and relaxation techniques. Input from the sports psychologist is not only needed, but requisite in the rehabilitation process.

This paper will discuss some of the competencies of the SPT from a theoretical background and will try to develop its related practical consequences, not only from the point of view of a practitioner, but also in an educational context. It is clear that some difficulties in general related to the basic education of the physical therapist and sports physical therapist in particular, and concerning research done in this area, still exist. This may jeopardize the extent of the discipline's professionalism and competence - especially when one claims to be a sports physical therapy specialist!

Attributed competencies

The sports physical therapist, characterized as being the „masseur" of the team, carrying a „magic" bag stuffed with pouches, rolls of tape and bandages, is an image that many have. The competencies of the SPT are often attributed mostly to the contents of his or her bag.

Although nowadays things might look a little bit different, the competency of the SPT is mostly influenced by the health care culture of the individual country, the financial means of the federation/team/athlete, the acceptance by the sports medical professionals, and other more subjective matters. However, in recent years, the SPT seems to comprise more and/or other competencies, but achieving a consensus to delineate responsibilities still proved to be difficult.

An example one could bring into consideration is the competency statement made within the American Physical Therapy Association (Zachachewski et al., 1994). These competencies are summarized in Table 1. The results of the survey demonstrated that the most important competency is considered to be the evaluation (i.e. physical examination) to provide an accurate physical diagnosis of the musculoskeletal injury, which is the backbone of appropriate rehabilitation program prescription. Performing the necessary assessments and spending a great deal of time in assessing is recognized by SPT's as being the prerequisite for a successful rehabilitation program. The SPT has to select the appropriate diagnostic tools, both subjective and objective, with which he or she can determine the severity of the injury. The evaluation comprises the implementation of functional tests for status and progression documentation purposes. The diagnostic tools may vary to include questioning, „subjective" manual tests, goniometry, manual muscle testing, to more sophisticated assessment techniques, such as isokinetic dynamometry, kinesiological electromyograpy and other computer aided techniques. Furthermore, the understanding of medical imaging techniques is an important aid with respect to the determination of the severity of the injury. It must be realized that although many of the evaluation techniques available are of clinical relevance, many questions still remain open regarding their reliability, validity and sensitivity (e.g. concerning isokinetic dynamometry, see below).

The results of these tests are important to decide when the athlete is able to return to sporting activities and to provide feedback to the treating physician, to the coach, parents and administrators for counseling purposes. However, it goes without saying that the SPT is bound to professional ethics as to which information is handed over to whom. Furthermore, the SPT, as in other areas of physical therapy, should not focus the assessment on the impairment only (loss of strength), but should be able to evaluate the resulting functional limitations (restrictions in basic actions) and the related disability (difficulty in performing), as was suggested by Verbrugge and Jette (1993).

The rehabilitation programs administered are in the first place physical interventions. One of the major aims is to provide means to regain competitive condition as soon as possible, and to „bridge the gap" between athlete (performance and health related issues), sports physician (health related issues) and trainer or coach (performance related issues), as already mentioned above. Methods like manual therapy, massage, electrotherapy and taping are but limited examples of available conventional physical therapeutic tools. Furthermore, exercise prescription, be it training therapy, functional training, proprioceptive and kinesthetic training, and so on, also belong to the rehabilitative competency of the SPT, and constitute the majority of time spent in a therapy session. Exercise modalities and intensities may be increased as a function of the individual patient status and the phase of healing of the injured tissues which determine loading capacities. The final phase of the functional rehabilitation program, is again determining when the athlete is ready to resume participation in sports (Lephart & Henry, 1995).

One cannot deny that during the whole rehabilitation process, the education of the patient is an important factor contributing to the progress of his/her physical performance. Non-compliance with the rehabilitation program, frequently due to the athlete's anxiety or frustration, still remains a significant problem preventing effective recovery (Ford & Gordon, 1997).

With respect to intervention on the field (training, game, competition), in many cases the SPT is responsible for the initial (emergency) care just after the injury has occurred . Recognizing the extent of the injury and determining whether the athlete may or may not continue his/her activities without further harm, is often attributed to the competency of the SPT, in the absence of any other more qualified professional health care provider. He or she will also be responsible for the management, transport and eventual referral of the patient to other emergency care providers.

Furthermore, educating athletes, as well as coaches, administrators, and relatives is also one of the duties recognized by the sports physical therapy professionals, not only for rehabilitation purposes, but also from the standpoint of injury prevention (secondary prevention). Here, the SPT tries to bridge a gap between the medical team (surgeon, MD), the sports team (coach, members of the team, club), the human environment of the individual (supporters, press, relatives) on the one hand and the individual athlete/ patient on the other. Patient education and information, for example, has been recognized as one of the most important factors contributing to successful regaining of normal (and athletic) function. This information may be of various kinds, such as informal lectures and conversations, up to more formal interventions such as, for example, 'back schools'. However, practical experience teaches us that most of this information is transmitted during the actual therapeutic sessions. Therefore, psychological skills training and learning to deal with psychological responses to injury, if incorporated into the training of the SPT, would facilitate more effective treatment (Ford & Gordon, 1997).

Theoretical backgrounds concerning SPT education

The theoretical backgrounds of sports physiotherapy are multiple. They range from different areas in sports medicine (e.g. sports traumatology, exercise immunology, wound healing processes, indications and contra-indications, and so on) and sports science (biomechanics, exercise physiology, training methods, and so on) to specific techniques used in physiotherapy (e.g. mobilization, taping, electrotherapy, medical training therapy, etc.). Inclusion of these and other areas has the primary aim of providing the physical therapist with an advanced level of knowledge both in theoretical backgrounds and clinical skills, rather than a rudimentary level.

Knowledge concerning the specific characteristics of the movement of a particular sport (i.e. kinesiology, movement analysis, sports biomechanics, sports psychology, and other sports sciences) may be regarded as the basis from which the sports physical therapist will propose an individual program for the athlete, bearing in mind the basic knowledge of the healing processes of the damaged tissues, the condition of the athlete, and the stage of injury repair and recovery. Specifically, knowledge of healing processes for damaged tissues, of the athlete's condition and stage of injury repair and recovery are regarded as fundamental for a successful treatment (i.e. immunology, tissue physiology, wound healing physiology). According to the physiological processes described, the degree of tissue loading will be determined, so that loading capacities of the healing tissues are not compromised.

Areas such as sports traumatology (injury mechanisms, epidemiology), medical imaging techniques, nutrition physiology, muscle and exercise physiology, and so on are of course of importance to the SPT not only from a theoretical point of view (e.g. for risk factor recognition), but as basic contributions to practical applications in rehabilitation and injury prevention.

However, it must be stated that in many cases, the available knowledge is far from sufficient to enable higher education teaching, because of the structure of basic education. Furthermore, the danger of becoming outdated through lack of self-initiative and the reluctance of many to acquire and assimilate new information (through scientific literature, the internet, and other sources) has become a reality and may lead to an unprofessional attitude. Additionally, understanding and interpreting research results require knowledge of research methodology and statistics, and are important for new therapeutic insights, based on hard evidence. The fact that many complain about misunderstandings and rivalry of other health care providers is due mostly to misunderstandings created by SPT's themselves. Therefore, communication skills are not only important for rehabilitation and prevention purposes, but also should be used for marketing the profession with respect to other disciplines. This will prevent many of the existing competency conflicts the SPT is confronted with in daily practice.

Practical consequences: the use of isokinetic equipment in the assessment and rehabilitation process of sports performance and injuries.

This example of a strength assessment and rehabilitation method will be used to point out some of the educational consequences new technologies have offered the SPT.

The use of isokinetic equipment in the assessment and training of muscular strength and the rehabilitation of musculoskeletal injuries has become popular in the last two decades. Especially welcome has been its power to document rehabilitation progress, but this has often been overemphasized in practice.

Isokinetics is a movement condition, in which the angular velocity is kept constant and the resistance is accommodated to the force developed by the user. Since the introduction of isokinetic equipment, many applications in the field of sports medicine have been developed for reasons of assessment (e.g. before injury, for the prevention of injuries), strength training (e.g. for adjusting training programs), and intervention control (e.g. pre- and post rehabilitation).

The isokinetic parameters used to evaluate the athlete's effort are somewhat confusing: peak force, peak torque, power and work are the most commonly used, as well as left/right (involved/uninvolved) and agonist/ antagonist ratios (Cabri, 1991). However, recent literature has pointed out that the use of hybrid parameters is known to be most unreliable and does not contribute to validity (Gleeson & Mercer, 1996, Pincivero et al., 1997). Furthermore, in the healthy elite athlete, isokinetic parameters have not proven to be sensitive enough to detect training influences (Murphy & Wilson, 1997). Therefore, more practical tests (i.e. related to the specific requirements of the individual sport) should be implemented in the sport-specific evaluation of athlete's performances.

A valuable feature of isokinetic exercise is that the amount of resistance produced by the equipment is directly related to the amount of force the exercising muscle group is producing on the machine (accommodated resistance). Furthermore, through the use of biofeedback, both the therapist and the patient have a tool to monitor the forces produced in real-time. These and other possibilities provide a relatively safe way to exercise and rehabilitate strength, in both an open or closed kinetic chain. However, it should be mentioned that training on isokinetic equipment is velocity dependent and thus a wide spectrum of angular velocities should be advocated as soon as possible. Additionally, isokinetic equipment should be used only as long as the patient is not able to perform more functional exercises for reasons of protecting the injured structure. Therefore, isokinetic exercise is only one phase in a more complex rehabilitation program.

The information stated above, which is based on solid scientific research may be important for the SPT to realize not to jump too rapidly to easy conclusions using newly developed equipment. However, the fact that isokinetic exercise has some advantages over other forms of strength training techniques does not automatically imply that it may be used in all circumstances or conditions. Training isokinetically also has some disadvantages, which are not always mentioned (velocity specificity, angle specificity, joint reaction forces, amongst others) and which should be included in the education of SPT's. It is therefore important for the professional to be informed on a regular basis either through „lifelong continuing education" or through reading relevant literature. The latter is often considered to be more of a burden than a relief!

Conclusions

Sports physical therapy is a specialty within the profession of physical therapy which is earning its place in the sports medical team. Evidence based interventions focused on assessment (evaluation), rehabilitation and prevention are regarded as the major competencies of the SPT. Therefore, education in sports physical therapy should be focused on new developments in these areas, too. This will improve the quality of the profession, as measured through clinical outcomes. However, much research still needs to be performed in order to provide strong proof of these interventions.

Bibliography

1. Cabri J (1991) Isokinetic strength aspects in human joints and muscles, Applied Ergonomics 22(5): 299-302.
2. Ford, I. and Gordon, S. (1997) Perspective of sport physiotherapists on the frequency and significance of psychological factors in professional practice: implications for curriculum design in professional training, Aus J Sci Med Sport, 29:2, 34-40.
3. Gleeson, N and Mercer, T. (1996), The utility of isokinetic dynamometry

in the assessment of human muscle function, Sports Med, 21:1, 18-34.

4. Murphy, A. and Wilson, G. (1997) The ability of muscular function to reflect training-induced changes in performance, J Sports Scie, 15, 191-200.

5. Lephart, S. and Henry, T. (1995) Functional rehabilitation for the upper and lower extremity, Orthop Clin North Am, 26:3, 579-592.

6. Pincivero, D., Lephart, S. and Karunaka, R. (1997) Reliability and precision of isokinetic strength and muscular endurance for the quadriceps and hamstrings, Int. J. Sports Med., 18:2, 113-117.

7. Verbrugge, L and Jette, M (1993), The disablement process, Soc. Sci Med, 38:1, 1-14.

8. Zachazewski, J., Felder, C., Knortz, K., Thein, L. and Quillen, W. (1994) Competency revalidation study: a description of advanced clinical practice in sports physical therapy, JOPT, Vol. 20, 110-124.

13

SPORTS MEDICINE IN THE EUROPEAN UNION IN CONSIDERATION WITH THE SITUATION IN AUSTRIA

P. BAUMGARTL
Institute for Sports Medicine St. Johann in Tyrol

Keywords: Austria, education program, EV, FIMS, LMGSM, NWEC, sports medicine.

In the European union (EU) there exists a tendency to establish sports medicine as a special branch. The greatest difficulty consists not only in greatly differing educational programs between the individual member countries, but in most of these countries there also exist very distinct possibilities for sports medical education.

In 3 countries - Finland, Italy and the Netherlands - a specialization in sports medicine is possible; the education program has a duration of 4 years and is exactly defined. The practical education, i.e. working with the athlete and teams or sports associations, is of fundamental importance in addition to learning sports medical theory.

In some countries it is possible to learn different fields of sports medicine already as a student at university; in other countries, as in Austria, this is not available.

One will subsequently find a schedule of the different sports-medical education systems regarding the two subgroups of the World Sports Medicine Association (FIMS), namely the North West European Chapter (NWEC) and the Latin and Mediterranean Group of Sports Medicine (LMGSM), respectively. These 2 groups have not harmonized very well, in part due to language difficulties and in part due to other reasons. With the establishing of the European Society of Sports Medicine (ESSM), into which all European countries are integrated, it is hoped that co-operation will improve according to the intention of the EU including for candidates of an EU expansion and "the rest of Europe".

The precondition for obtaining a sports medical credential requires either three years general practice training as a physician or specialization in a medicine specialty with an average duration of about 6 years. The candidate therefore has the possibility of receiving a sports medicine certification or a diploma. There exist different systems of education in European countries operating at various levels; on the other hand, there exists a possibility of a superspecializing, i.e. a specialist for a certain medial subject receives intensive sports medical education in the subject for approximately 3 years. Last but not least in some EU countries, specialization in sports medicine per se is also available.

Sports Medical Education in the North West European Chapter (NWEC) of FIMS:

1 Belgium:
   1 or 2 years of post-graduate study in sports medicine organized by universities.

2 Denmark:
   Sports medical education organized by the Danish Association of Sports Medicine and the University of Copenhagen.
   a) Basic course: 40-50 hours (step 1): 1 week 3 times a year
   b) Advanced course: 40-50 hours (step 2): special themes 1 week a year respectively
   c) Specialized course: 20 hours (step 3): e.g. endocrinology, shoulder traumatology etc; organized in collaboration with Norway and Sweden with a duration of 3-5 days at a time.

3 Germany:
   Diploma of the German Sports Medical Association (DSÄB):
   DSÄB bestows on request a diploma should the candidate fulfill the following conditions in the local country's sports medical association:
   1. Membership in one of the local associations of the German Sports Medical Association
   2. Approbation as a physician
   3.a. 90 hours additional education in physical exercise and sports medicine at symposia recognized by the DSÄB, including
        a a: at least 45 hours in the theory and practice of physical exercise
        a b: at least 45 hours of additional sports medical education.

   Alternatively to 3a there exists the following possibility of additional education:
   3.b. At least a half year's work in a sports medical institution or a sports medical clinic.

Undergraduate sports medical programs are recognized up to 60 hours.

Additional "Sports Medicine" Designation:

The additional "sports medicine" title is bestowed by local physician chambers to physicians after general practical training if they fulfill the following conditions:

1.   2 year clinical post-graduate course (1 year all-day postgraduate education in co-operation with an authorized physician)
2.1. 1 year whole-day post-graduate education at a sports medical institution under the leadership of an authorized physician.

Alternatively to 2.1.:

2.2.1. Participation in an introductory course in the theory of physical exercise (120 hours). The course must be acknowledged by the chamber of physicians.
2.2.2. Participation in a sports medical course with a duration of 120 hours (recognized by the chamber of physicians)
2.2.3. 1 year practical sports medical work with a sports team or sports association.

Additionally determinations of exact practicability exist, but a precise description is not possible within the scope of this paper. All possibilities for sports medical education in Germany are completely defined.

The title "sports physician" in the old federal districts of Germany did not exist, and no one is allowed to bear this title !

4   Finland:

There exists an undergraduate program for students in sports medicine. Before starting the postgraduate sports medical educational program a 2-year working period as a physician must be completed. Education for specializing in sports medicine takes 4 years, including 6 months clinical physiology and 6 months surgery, and additionally an obligatory 2.5-3 year working period in a sports medical research station. During these educational periods a thesis in sports medicine may be written; however, it is not obligatory.

Sports medical specialization courses are operated by some universities in co-operation with the Finnish sports medical association. Specialization in sports medicine has the same standing as specializations in internal medicine, surgery or pediatrics etc.

5 Great Britain:
   Various university clinics offer widely differing educational programs, for instance the London Hospital Medical College offers a 1 year continuous course which ends with an examination for a sports medical diploma. A collaboration with the Crystal Palace clinic for sports injuries exists; additionally a 2 year MSc course in sports medicine is available. Similar possibilities can be found in the universities of Nottingham, Edinburgh, Glasgow and Bath University. On the other hand a modular education system exists and correspondence courses for MSc in sports medicine for physicians, physiotherapists and sports scientists are available. In Great Britain there are at the moment 3 professors for sports medicine.

6 Ireland:
   Various systems also exist in Ireland . The Royal College of Surgeons arranges a 9 month training course for sports medicine, a whole year course to obtain a MSc is arranged at Trinity College in Dublin. The MSc title in sports medicine can be obtained also at the University of Cork; the University of Dublin offers 1 year to achieve a sports medical diploma. Additionally some "part-time courses" and similar facilities are available.

7 The Netherlands:
   In the Netherlands a sports medicine specialty program is available after a four year education program. 1 year cardiology, 1 year orthopedics, 6 months physiology and 4 months practice is essential. Training courses are available during residency in a hospital, and a module system offers an additional possibility in sports medical education. At the moment in Holland there is one professor for sports medicine.

8 Sweden:
   In Sweden there exists the same system as in Denmark and Norway (not an EU member); additionally there are university courses in Umea and Stockholm over a period of 20 weeks, and shorter courses over 1 to 3 weeks in Uppsala and Lund are available.
   Additionally in Sweden an authorization in sports medicine is possible, granted by the Swedish Society of Sports Medicine in connection with the Swedish Sports Federation and the Swedish Olympic Committee. In this case 1 year of sports medical practice is necessary.
   It is possible to work 6 months in a sports medical department.

In Sweden at the moment there are 3 professors for sports medicine.

Austria is also integrated into the North West European Chapter of FIMS, and about our country I will report later.

Latin and Mediterranean Group of Sports Medicine in the FIMS:

1 France
   Since 1949 there exists the possibility of acquiring a sports medical diploma in France which can be completed after 1 year by written, verbal and additionally practical examinations. Since 1988 there exists a certification for proof of qualification in medicine and sports biology which consists of a theoretical section with 100-120 hours and a practical section with a minimum of 40 half days. These courses are organized by various medical faculties and are financially sponsored by the state's Secretary for Youth, Sport and Leisure. Additionally there are various inter-university diplomas, mainly in traumatology and pathology of the skeletal and muscular system, especially offered by the universities of Nice, Marseille, Lyon and Paris. This diploma is available after a 1 year course (with examination), but obviously does not have the standing of the "proof of qualification" for medicine and sports biology.

2 Greece:
   In this country there exist no definite educational guidelines, but physicians of various disciplines with different scientific expertise in sports medicine are active in the field of sports medicine. Since 1979 there is a center for sports medical research with its own antidoping section.

3 Italy:
   Like other medical disciplines in Italy sports medicine is regional. Recently, a complete education organized in different ways comes to 4 years. A "numerus clausus" or restricted enrollment already exists for beginning this special education. Preferred are colleagues with a sport background. Required are an admission examination, a frequency record, examinations every year and at the end a thesis.
   Training courses over 4 years are exactly defined and contain all the main subjects as well as the border lands of sports medicine; the necessary 800 hours are exactly subdivided.

Italy at the moment is surely the EU's best developed country in sports medicine with 16 professorships for sports medicine.

4 Luxembourg:
    In Luxembourg it is possible to obtain special education in sports medicine after medical graduation; a credential of sports medical education obviously does not exist at the moment.

5 Portugal:
    1. Post-graduate-course in sports medicine (duration: 12 months)
    2. Education which is officially acknowledged by the Portuguese Sports Medicine College in a sports medical center in the following subjects:
       sports medicine: 12 months *
       orthopedic surgery - traumatology: 4 months
       physical medicine and rehabilitation: 3 months
       performance physiology: 4 months
       clinical pathology and toxicology: 1 month
       practice in a medical department of an institute of sports science: 12 months

       * The sports medical courses must include instruction in surgery, cardiology and pneumology.

6 Spain:
    Courses for the sports medicine diploma are regularly conducted at the universities of Madrid, Barcelona and Oviedo. The duration of the courses is 3 years, totaling 600 hours, out of which 535 hours are reserved for basic subjects of sports medicine. Spain co-operates very closely with Italy and is thus far linked very much to the Italian standard, except that the duration of the training courses is 1 year shorter.

The sports medical situation in Austria

At the moment in Austria there exist 2 levels of sports medical education. The diploma for sports medicine issued by the Austrian chamber of physicians contains 120 hours of theory and 60 hours of practice which must be completed within 3 years and accepted by the Department for Sports Medicine and Sport Physicians of the Austrian Chamber of Physicians. The contents of the complete training program are worked out by the Austrian society of sports medicine. Training in theory is divided on the one hand into a 40 hour basic course in the subject of internal/physiological sports medicine (4 blocks à 10 hours) and on the other into a 40 hour basic course (4 blocks à 10 hours) in orthopedic-traumatologic-physical sports medicine.

The remaining 40 hours of sports medical theory is divided into special themes which derive from the first 2 blocks - in this area questions concerning sports psychology and prophylaxis and questions concerning sports buildings, sports outfit, gymnastic apparatus theory, organization and other specialized subjects of sports medicine are taught.

60 practical hours are divided into 40 hours of practical seminars, which are exactly defined, and 20 hours of sport for physicians (active practice under the guidance of a coach or instructor).

Working with a team during the last half year prior to receiving the diploma is required and good standing independently as a physician is of course also necessary to receive the ÖÄK-diploma in sports medicine.

Should the training courses for the ÖÄK-diploma for sports medicine be completed before the standard of ius practicandi, 10 additional hours of theory must be completed until the right of independent professional activity is given.

For maintenance of the diploma, continuing sports medical training courses are necessary: proof of 20 hours theory every 3 years, basic courses count only half of the amount of actual hours and practice seminars only up to 5 hours.

In Austria at the moment there are 725 holders of the diploma, and these physicians are allowed to use the additional "sports medicine" title. To date an examination is not necessary.

A 2nd level is possible with a type of superspecializing after having specialized in internal medicine, traumatology, orthopedic surgery and physical medicine. Over the 3 year period, a defined training system is required. The courses can be booked at sports medical university institutes and various institutes for sports medicine acknowledged as official bodies. Unfortunately at the moment in Austria temporary rules for some years exist which reduce the value of those "additional specializations". At the moment in our country there are 92 sports traumatologists, 30 sports orthopedic surgeons, 19 internal sports physicians and 11 sports physicalists (state: 31.12.1997).

A specialization in "medical physiology of performance" is itself counted as a medical specialization; at the moment there are 4 specialists for medical physiology of performance in Austria.

There are 30 sports medical institutions spread out over the whole of

Austria and officially mentioned in the Austrian Journal of Sports Medicine. These are situated mainly in larger cities, but distributed over all 9 federal districts.

In Styria there exists an extraordinary situation as 8 of 9 institutions for sports medicine are located in the capital (Graz). In this case less could be sometimes more, but mainly political reasons lead to inappropriate competition (3 political holding companies have their own institute for sports medicine).

In Austria sport is an affair of the 9 federal districts, and therefore payment for sports medical work in the different districts varies widely. At the moment in Tyrol a solution is being prepared; in Vienna no plan exists thus far. Discussion with participation of sport federations and athletes about various payment models with different suggestions within the framework of payment through the support of different districts, the federal government and the national health system should find a common solution for the entire state.

The "Institution for Sports Scientific and Sports Medical Consultation" (formerly a project and then an association) arranges courses in theory and practice and provides some satellite institutions in several districts with a certain level of financial assistance.

In Austria it is a severe loss that the medical faculties of the universities are not interested in sports medicine - no courses for students or post-graduate courses exist. In contrast to university activities in sports science, most physicians need to practice sports medicine "incidentally" besides their regular work with their standard patients, mostly during their off-time. This renders research in sports medicine more difficult; the few district institutes for sports medicine are blocked up by routine work, without enough staff and without enough time to work together with their athletes in training and competition. Unfortunately due to these reasons it is not possible to collaborate with sports science institutes in an adequate way.

The professorship for sports physiology in Vienna, which is not included in the medical faculty, has the opportunity to work in sports medical research; the personnel situation allows only in part efficient care of teams and individual athletes in training and competition. This institute is connected with the Austrian Institute of Sports Medicine (ÖISM).

In Austria the following goals concerning sports medicine should be fought for:

1. At universities sports medical courses should be held for students as well as post-graduate courses.

2. Professorships for sports medicine should be established at Austrian universities; enough medical and paramedical staff should be employed at these institutes to tend to individual athletes and teams during periods of training and competition .

3. Integration of sports medicine into BSO (Bundessportorganisation - Federal Sports Organization), into the various sport federations and the NOC of Austria. On the other hand sports medical support of Olympic efforts should be established as they already exist in many EU-countries; for organizing regular care for top athletes in medical and physiotherapeutic aspects, close co-operation with sports science institutes is of great importance.

   The Obertauern "Olympic support base" is a private organization and, given an appropriate gathering of staff and instruments, should act as an example for other similar institutions in the future.

4. In Austria there should be established one unique system of payment for sports medical services with exactly designated payment schedules for sports medical work as well for the physician in a sports medical practice, at sports medical institutes and for sports medical care in training and competitions .

5. Adjustment of post-graduate educational systems to the EU-standard; a minimum of 4 years sports medical education should be completed and capped by an examination.

Conclusion

It will not be easy for coordinators in Brussels to find a unique solution for sports medical education in the EU. I take the view that a minimum of a 4 year education in theoretical and practical sports medicine ending with an examination should be established. The definite organization of sports medical training and possibilities of care for teams and athletes should be a matter for each EU country according to sport's rank of importance and the financial situation of the member country.

Index of authors

Index of keywords

preparatory research
    51
process accompanying training
    51
profile
    146
psychology
    45, 129
rehabilitation
    32
research
    115, 129
resources
    32
role conflict
    146
running
    115
scientific support
    74
sensation seeking
    146
service
    66
ski jumping
    11, 82
soccer
    129
social interaction
    45
social network
    146
social sciences
    66
Spain
    115
sport physio-therapist
    163
sport specific movement
    163
sports medicine
    32, 74, 171
sports science
    74
sport-specific variables of influence
    11
strength training
    97
swimming
    115

technique-specific strength training
    11
tennis
    11, 115
test
    163
testing
    97
trainer
    45
training devices
    11
training science
    11
wrestling
    51